Right to Speedy Trial

Indian Judiciary and Justice Delivery System

Right to Speedy Trial

Indian Judiciary and Justice Delivery System

NUR MD. ABDULLAH AHMED MAJUMDAR
Sub-divisional Judicial Magistrate
Silchar, Cachar (Assam)

and

AHSAN RASHID
Assistant Professor
Central University of Bihar
(Bihar)

REGAL PUBLICATIONS
New Delhi

RIGHT TO SPEEDY TRIAL
Indian Judiciary and Justice Delivery System

ISBN 978-81-8484-438-2

Typeset by
RAHUL COMPOSERS
New Highway Apartments, Lakshmi Niwas
760, Pocket-D, Lok Nayak Puram, New Delhi - 110 041

Printed in India at
MAYUR ENTERPRISES
WZ Plot No. 3, Gujjar Market, Tihar Village, New Delhi - 110 018

Published by
REGAL PUBLICATIONS
F-159, Rajouri Garden, New Delhi - 110 027
Phone : 45546396, 25435369
E-mail : regalbookspub@yahoo.com, regaldeepbooks@yahoo.com

Contents

Preface

Indian judiciary is known for its impartiality, independence and justice-oriented approach. However recently, the capabilities and ways of functioning of Indian Judiciary were under challenge as a feeling of disillusionment and frustration was witnessed among the people of this country. The number of pending cases in the Supreme Court as on May 2014 is 63,843, an increase of 9% from 58,519 cases in 2011. Arrears of cases in courts, particularly in High Courts and District Courts, has been a cause of great concern for litigants as well as for the State. The situation of the pendency of cases is worst in the Subordinate Courts. As per available information, the pendency of cases in District/Subordinate Courts as on 31st December 2007 was 25.2 million cases, 27.6 million cases as per December 2012 data and which has now come to 20 million in 2013 registering a fall. While 4.4 million are pending in various high courts.

The biggest challenge being faced by the justice delivery system in India is that of delay in the dispensation of justice. Heavy back-log of cases in the Courts and inevitable delay in the dispensation of justice has been to such an extent that it is shaking public trust and confidence in the legal system and it is tending to erode the quality of social justice. The objective of legal system and the societal interest in setting the legal system in motion against the offenders with reasonable expedition is thereby frustrated. The adverse effect of delay on the society at large is immeasurable. The fear of law and the faith in the judicial system is eroded irretrievably. It is a fundamental right of every citizen to get speedy justice and speedy trial which also is the fundamental requirement of good judicial administration. In this book, we have made efforts to evaluate and assess the justice delivery system in India, to discuss and analyze the constitutionality of the right to speedy trial, the reason behind the pendency of the cases, to evaluate the judicial approach to speedy trial and to ascertain the impediments behind speedy trial and also to suggest ways and means to ensure speedy trial.

These endeavors would be proposed to be secured mainly by analyzing the judicial behavior and trends based on the judgments by the Supreme Court as well as High Courts. Further, the suggestions and recommendations given from time to time by various committees and commissions including the reports of law commission is also considered.

NUR MD. ABDULLAH AHMED MAJUMDAR
AHSAN RASHID

Table of Cases

Abdul Rahman Antulay *v.* R.S. Nayak, (1992) 1 SCC 225
Abinandan Jha *v.* Dinesh Mishra, AIR 1968 SC 117, 120; 1968 Cri LJ 97
Ahmad Ilahi *v.* State, (08/09/2003), 2003(6) AD (Del) 599
Akhtari Bi *v.* State of Madhya Pradesh, (2001) 4 SCC 355
All India Judges' Association *v.* Union of India, (2002) 4 SCC 247
Anirudha Bahal's Case 172 (2010) Delhi Law Times 268
Anil Rai *v.* State of Bihar, AIR 2001 SC 3173
Barker *v.* Wingo, 33 L Ed 2d 101
Beavers *v.* Henkel, 194 US 73 (1904)
Bell *v.* Director of Prosecution, Jamaica, (1985) 2 All ER 585
Betts *v.* Baddy, 316 US 455 (1942)
Bivens *v.* Agents of the Federal Bureau of Narcotics, 403 U.S. 388 (1971)
Bounds *v.* Smith, 430 U.S. 817 (1977)
Brewer *v.* Williams, 430 US 387 (1977)
Cawford *v.* Washington, 541 US 36 (2004)
Chajoo Ram *v.* Radhey Shayam, AIR 1971 SC 1367
Charles Sobhraj *v.* Suptd., Central Jail, Tihar (1979) I.S.C.R 514-515
"Common Cause" a Registered Society through its Director *v.* Union of India, (1996) 4 SCC 3
Diwan Naubat Rai *v.* State through Delhi Administration
Dr. Subramanian Swamy *v.* Dr. Manmohan Singh, 2012 (2) SCALE 12
Durga Datta Sharma *v.* State, 2004(1) Crimes 171
Faretta *v.* California, 368 US 52 (1961)
Godinez *v.* Moran, 509 U.S. 389 (1993)

Hamilton *v.* Alabama, 422 U.S. 806 (1975)
H.N. Rishbud *v.* State of Delhi, AIR 1955 SC 196
Hussainara Khatoon *v.* Home Secretary, State of Bihar (1980) 1 SCC 81
Henderson *v.* United States, 476 US 321(330) (1986)
Imtiyaz Ahmed *v.* State of U.P., 18 2012(2) SCALE 81
Janta Dal *v.* H.S. Chaudhary (1992) 4 SCC 305
Janhit Manch *v.* UOI, W.P. (C) No. 122 of 2008
Jhonson *v.* Zerbst, 287 US 45 (1932),
Kadra Pahadiya *v.* State of Bihar, (1983) 2 SCC 104: 1983 SCC (Cri) 361
Kartar Singh *v.* State of Punjab, (1994) 3 SCC 569
Klopfer *v.* North Carolina, 386 US 213(1967)
Machander *v.* State of Hyderabad, AIR 1955 SC 792
Madhav Rao Jivaji Rao Scindia *v.* Sambhaji Rao Chandroji Rao, AIR 1988 SC 709
Madhu Mehta *v.* Union of India, (1989) 4 SCC 62
Malik Mazhar Sultan *v.* Union Public Service Commission, C.A. No. 1867 of 2006
Maneka Gandhi *v.* Union of India, (1978) 1 SCC 248
Mihir Kumar *v.* State of West Bengal, 1990 Cr LJ 26 (Cal)
M.V. Chauhan *v.* State of Gujarat, AIR 1997 SC 3400
N.S. Sahni *v.* Union of India, (2002) 2 SCC 210
Powell *v.* Alabama, 287 U.S. 45 (1932)
Raghubir Singh *v.* State of Bihar, (1986) 4 SCC 481: AIR 1987 SC 149
Raj Deo Sharma *v.* State of Bihar, A.I.R 1998 SC 3281
Rajiv Gupta *v.* State of Himachal Pradesh, (2000) 10 SCC 68
R.D. Upadhyay *v.* State of Andhra Pradesh, (1996) 3 SCC 422
Rakesh Saxena *v.* State through C.B.I. (1986) 3 SCC 505
Sachidanand Pandey *v.* State of West Bengal, AIR 1987 SC 1109
Salem Advocate Bar Association, Tamilnadu *v.* Union of India, AIR 2005 SC 3353
Sangram Singh *v.* Election Tribunal, AIR 1955 SC 425
Santosh De *v.* Arachana Guha, AIR 1994 SC 1229
Sheela Barse *v.* Union of India (1986) 3 SCC 632
S.P. Gupta *v.* Union of India, AIR 1982 SC149
Srinivas Pal *v.* Union Territory of Arunachal Pradesh, (1988) 4 SCC 36
State of West Bengal *v.* Anwar Ali Sarkar, AIR 1952 SC 75.
State of Uttar Pradesh *v.* Kapil Deo Shukla (1972) 3 SCC 504

1

Introduction

"If I were asked to mention the greatest drawback of the administration of justice in India today I would say it is delay in the disposal of cases".

—Late Nani A. Palkhivala, Famous Jurist

"Quality of justice suffers not only when an innocent person is punished or a guilty person is exonerated but when there is enormous delay in deciding the criminal cases".

—Committee on Reforms of Criminal Justice System

1. THEMATIC APPROACH

Judiciary in independent India is the most important institution for it has been entrusted with the job ranging from redressing the grievances of common man to resolving disputes between the Union and the States, as also between States *inter se* arising mainly for want of legal interpretation of the Constitution and various laws. Judiciary is envisaged as the third pillar of the democratic system in which the masses have faith as the protector of their Fundamental Rights. Of late, certain irregularities have crept in the judicial system and the arrears of cases in the Courts have attracted much attention due to their sheer magnitude and put a question mark on the efficacy of the judiciary because justice has to be associated with timely redressal to realize its true meaning. This is probably the reason for the phrase **"Justice Delayed Is Justice Denied"** to assume axiomatic proportions.

Inordinate delays in the investigation and prosecution of criminal cases involving serious offences, and in the trial of such cases in the Courts is a blot on justice system. The objective of penal law and the societal interest in setting the criminal law in motion against the offenders with reasonable expedition is thereby defeated. The adverse effect of delay on the society at large is immeasurable. The fear of law and faith in the criminal justice system is eroded irretrievably.

The case referred to in this Writ Petition is an extreme example of the slow-motion of criminal justice process and the extent to which it can be subverted. It unfolds the apparent apathy on the part of all those concerned with administration of criminal justice. The fact that influential political personalities and their henchmen are involved in this case presents an added dimension to the issue and raises questions on the efficacy of the existing systems and practices to counter the moves of such influential persons facing serious criminal charges.[1]

Public interest demands that the criminal cases, especially those related to serious crimes are concluded within a reasonable time so that the guilty are punished. Further, from the point of view of the accused also, the right to speedy trial is a fundamental right. People get frustrated by the system, if at every stage, there is delay and the process of justice is not allowed to take its normal course, more so, when deliberate attempts are made to subvert and delay the process. Further, with the long passage of time, whatever evidence is there, it will vanish or eclipse. Oral evidence, which in most of the cases, is vital to the prosecution, will take a devious or distorted course. Hostile witnesses and witnesses with faded memories will be writ large in the system, with the long passage of time. Heavy reliance on oral evidence has telling drawbacks. Lack of expertise and sustained effort in investigation and non utilization of scientific methods of investigation is resulting in low rate of convictions and even implication of innocent persons.

Before the specifics of the problem are discussed, it would be useful to refer to certain data touching on the general scenario of criminal justice in the country with special reference to cases pending in the District and Subordinate (D&S) courts.

The total number of criminal cases pending before D&S Courts is about 1.90 crore (190 lakh) cases, about 82.25 lakhs civil cases are pending. That means, the number of criminal cases is about 2.50 times more than civil cases. The largest number of criminal cases are from the States of UP, Maharashtra, West Bengal, Gujarat, Bihar, Rajasthan and Odisha.[2] In 12 States, out of which there are eight major States, the disposals are less than the institutions.

However, on the whole, the institutions and disposals are almost matching in the year 2010. Out of the pending criminal cases, about 25% of the cases are pending for five years and more in many States.

At the end of the year 2010, 72.58 lakh cognizable criminal cases under IPC were pending trial[3] and 48.54 lakh cognizable criminal cases under Special and Local Laws were pending trial.[4] Trials were concluded in about 55.88 lakh cases (both IPC & SLL cases) during that year.

As challenges go, the justice system in India is up against it staring at more than 31.3 million pending cases. This backlog takes a toll on individuals as well as the system. Even the top is heavy in this case. The number of pending cases (civil + criminal) in the Supreme Court as on May 2014 is 63,843, an increase of 9% from 58,519 cases in 2011. The Supreme Court website states that more than 50% of the pending cases are miscellaneous and not ready regular hearing matters. Pending cases in high courts as on December 2013 stood at 4.4 million, up from 4.3 million in 2011. The Allahabad high court alone accounted for a million of these pending cases. The pendency of cases in district and subordinate courts was 20 million in 2013, registering a fall of 100,000 from 2011. Uttar Pradesh and Maharashtra have the highest backlog. Incidentally, UP is the most populous state in India and Maharashtra too has a huge population. Gujarat, not among the five most populous states in India, has the third highest number of pending cases in its district and subordinate courts. Incidentally, around 25% of cases in all courts are pending for five years or more 70% are pending for less than five years and the rest are instituted every year. Parliament data state that increasing number of legislations, accumulation of first appeals, adjournments and lack of logistics are the causes for more than 30 million cases pending.

Vacancies of judges and judicial personnel have also not helped. A closer look at the data reveals that the Supreme Court has five vacancies; high courts have 319, while district and subordinate courts have vacancies of 4382 judicial officers. We can see a correlation between vacancy of judges and pending number of cases in Allahabad and Calcutta high courts. The Allahabad high court has the highest number of vacancies as well as the highest number of pending cases. The Parliament recently passed the National Judicial Appointments Commission (NJAC) Bill that gives it power to regulate judicial appointments. At present, the judge strength is around 14 to 16 for a million citizens. Ideally, as per the Supreme Court, it should be around 50 per million. Developed regions like Europe have more than 150 judges per million, while the United States has nearly 100 judges for the same number. A possible way out could be the creation of more Lok Adalats. Between 2001 and 2012, a total of 104,728 Lok Adalats were conducted all across India and they disposed of more than 2.4 million cases. The National Mission for Justice Delivery and Legal Reforms was established in June 2011 with the primary aim of reducing delays. The Centre committed Rs. 5,510 crore for the mission from 2011-16. Efforts are on to tackle the challenge, but the piled up numbers suggest much more needs to be done, and fast.[5]

According to the data compiled by National Crime Records Bureau (NCRB), in its Publication relating to the year 2010, over 1.78 crore cognizable criminal cases, including cases registered under IPC and special/local laws (SLL), were pending for trial at the beginning of 2010 in various criminal courts.[6] 67.51 lakh cognizable crimes comprising 22.25 lakh IPC Crimes and 45.26 lakh crimes under SLL were reported in 2010.[7] The figures relating to cases pending trial do not apparently tally with the statistics shown in 'Court News' published by Supreme Court and the data furnished by the High Courts to Law Commission of India and this aspect is being rechecked.

6330 cases have been pending investigation from previous year under the Prevention of Corruption Act (PoCA) & related sections of the IPC in 2010 and 3822 cases were registered during the year. Therefore, a total of 10152 cases were pending investigation in 2010 out of which chargesheet was filed for 2929 cases.[8] In relation to these cases, 4578 persons were chargesheeted. Trial was completed for 3379 persons, out of whom 891 persons were convicted. Hence, the conviction rate *vis-à-vis* persons accused under PoCA in 2009 is 26.4%.[9]

Conviction rate in 2010 for violent crimes such as attempt to commit murder, rape, riots etc., is 27.7%. Conviction rate for crimes against women (IPC and SLL cases) for 2010 is 27.8%.[10] Conviction rate for all cognizable cases under IPC is 40.7%.[11]

In the State of Jharkhand (which needs special mention as specific reference has been made to that State in this W.P.), about 2.41 lakh criminal cases are pending. The total pendency of Civil and Criminal Cases in that State is about 2.93 lakh. Out of the Criminal cases, 60,500 including sessions cases are more than five years old. There were as many as 192 vacancies in District and Subordinate Judiciary in the State of Jharkhand as on 31st December, 2010. Year to year, the trend of increase in pendency of criminal cases including old cases is noticed except in a few States.

The total number of Jails (upto 2009) is 1374 and the total capacity of all jails in India is 3,07,052. However, the total number of inmates as on 31.12.2009 are 3,76,969. This shows that the number of jail inmates far exceeds the capacity of the jails in India. Out of them, 2,50,204 inmates representing 66.4% of the jail population are undertrial prisoners. Among them, the highest percentage (20%) of undertrials were charged with murder. 2422 (1%) undertrials were detained in jails for more than 5 years at the end of the year 2009.[12]

Trial of a case means the proceedings whereby the concerned parties put up their pleadings before the appropriate Court of Law for its consideration so as to arrive at a decision on the dispute. In a criminal trial, it is generally the state that institutes the case against the accused as crime is considered to be an offence against the whole society and not against one individual alone. Hence, it is the state that has on its shoulder the burden of investigation as well as prosecution in a criminal trial. All such trials have to be carried out as per the mandate of the law for the time being in force and according to the procedure prescribed under that law.

In a free society like ours, law is quite apprehensive of the personal liberty of every individual and doesn't tolerate the detention of any person without legal sanction. The right to personal liberty is a basic human right recognized by the General Assembly of the

United Nations in its Universal Declaration of Human Rights. This has also been prominently included in the convention on Civil and Political Rights, to which India is now a party. Indian Constitution under **Art. 21** recognizes it as a fundamental right. Art. 21 provides that "No person shall be deprived of his life or personal liberty except according to procedure established by law. Further, the procedure contemplated by this article must be 'right, just and fair' and not 'arbitrary, fanciful or oppressive; otherwise it would be no procedure at all.

1.1 Meaning and Concept of Speedy Trial

India achieved independence from Britain in 1947, and its constitution came into force in 1950. As noted above, the drafters did not include explicit language enshrining a defendant's right to a speedy trial.[13] Still the notion of under trial-prisoners being forced to serve extended periods of confinement was part of the Indian Supreme Court's discourse as early as 1952—albeit in a slightly unexpected manner. In Lachmandas Kewalram Ahuja, the Court held that defendants convicted under the pre-1950 criminal justice regime needed to have their rights conform to the new Constitution's fundamental guarantees.[14] In order to ensure their appearance at trial, however, the Court then ordered that the defendants "be retained in custody as under trial-prisoners,"[15] while the state prepared its new case.

Indeed, in the first two decades after independence, concern for the length of time under trial-detainees spent in prison did not seem to be a focus for the Court. On repeated occasions, the Court maintained a low threshold that the prosecution had to meet in order to justify the continued detention of under trial-prisoners.[16] Moreover, between 1975 and 1977, when the then Prime Minister Indira Gandhi suspended the Constitution and imposed Emergency Rule, the Court further buckled, caving to the government's demand specifically not to provide jailed political opponents and others with speedy trials.[17]

It was only after the lifting of the Emergency Rule and Mrs. Gandhi's resounding defeat in the following elections that the Court—in a concerted effort to regain, its legitimacy[18]—began fully examining the importance of not letting the incarcerated languish behind bars. The on-point decision in this regard came in the 1979 case of *Hussainara Khatoon* v. *Home Ministry*.[19] Written by arguably the most aggressive protector of individual liberties in the Court's post-Emergency period, Justice P.N. Bhagwati, the Hussainara Khatoon opinion established for the first time that a defendant had a fundamental right to a speedy trial under Article 21 of the Indian Constitution.[20] Fuelled by media accounts of the delays and horrendous conditions of various prisons, Justice Bhagwati's ruling ordered a massive revamping in how the prison population was to be treated by the state. In the decision, the Court mandated greater access to bail, more humane living standards, and a significant reduction in time from arrest to trial.[21] Furthermore, of comparative interest, the judgment referenced U.S. criminal procedure law in key sections.[22] It premised its rationale on a ruling from a year earlier, *Maneka Gandhi* v. *Union of India*.[23] With Justice Bhagwati also a main architect in that case, the Court stated that from that point forward substantive due process would be formally recognized as a fundamental aspect of the liberty provision of Article 21.[24]

Indian judiciary is known for its impartiality, independence and justice-oriented approach. However recently, the capabilities and ways of functioning of Indian Judiciary were under challenge as a feeling of disillusionment and frustration was witnessed among the people of this country. The biggest challenge being faced by the justice delivery system in India is that of delay in the dispensation of justice. Heavy back-log of cases in the Courts and inevitable delay in the dispensation of justice has been to such an extent that it is shaking public trust and confidence in the legal system and it is tending to erode the quality of social justice. So it is necessary to have speedy trial or speedy disposal of cases. By judicial interpretation and extension of the concept of personal liberty, the **'Right to Speedy Trial'** has been incorporated under **Art. 21**. But, it would be wrong to say that it is only by way of wide judicial interpretation of Art. 21 that the concept of speedy trial has been included under Art. 21 of our constitution, rather in its true sense, it is well-embedded in the term 'personal liberty'. By **speedy trial** we mean disposal of cases within a reasonable period of time. A procedure prescribed by law for depriving a person of his liberty cannot be termed as 'reasonable, fair and just' unless it ensures a speedy trial for determination of the guilt of the accused. Hence, the Supreme Court in *Hussainara Khatoon (iv)* v. *Home Secy, State of Bihar*[25] observed that "no procedure, which doesn't ensure a reasonably quick trial, be regarded as 'reasonable, fair and just' and it will be violative of Art 21 and hence is not valid under law. Breach of this fundamental right has the potential of making the entire prosecution liable to be quashed and closed. And the accused in all such cases will have to be declared innocent and set at large."

Thus, the personal liberty being the cornerstone of our social structure, speedy trial is the essence of criminal trial and there can be no doubt that a delay in trial *per se* constitutes denial of justice. Justice that comes too late has no meaning to the person it is meant for. During a prolonged and unending trial, the priorities of an accused person towards his life changes along with the circumstances. The person can also loose everything on account of the pending proceedings. Therefore, the speedy trial should be recognized as an urgent need of the present judicial system in order to decide the fate of lakhs of litigants. It will help to enhance the faith of general public in the judicial system. In cases where the accused is the head of a family and is the only bread earner, it is not only the accused but his other family members also who suffer because of delays in trial. Speedy trial ensures that a society is free of such vices. Speedy trial would also help save an accused from psychological stresses such as worries, anxiety, and disturbance to peace at home, etc. Speedy trial is, hence, a mandatory requirement as far as protecting the interest of an accused is concerned.

Uncalled delay often prejudices the prosecution and at times, witnesses are not available or evidences disappear by lapse of time due to various technical and non-technical reasons. When our Constitution has given us this fundamental right and our Supreme Court has recognized the same on more occasions than one, a realistic and practical approach should be adopted by all concerned to protect this integral right.

1.2 Pendency of Cases in various Courts

Coming to the facts in this regard, the numbers of pending cases at present amount to a staggering **31.3 million** in all the courts taken together in the country. There are cases where the disposal has taken as many as 30 to 40 years. The **Standing Committee of Home Affairs in its Report in 2007** relating to pendency of cases revealed the magnitude of the problem. Pendency of cases is spreading like epidemic, be it the Supreme Court, High Court or Subordinate Courts. That 73% of our total jail population are under-trials tell its own story of the griming situation of the pendency of cases.

As per latest available information, 57,179 cases were pending in the Supreme Court of India as on 30.6.11. The number of cases pending in the High Courts were 42,17,903 as on 30.9.2010; giving his information in written reply to a question in Rajya Sabha, Shri Salman Khurshid, Minister of Law & Justice informed the House.

A statistical presentation of the number of pending cases in the Supreme Court, High Courts and Subordinate Courts is given below:

Pendency in the Supreme Court

Long pendency of cases in the Supreme Court has become a matter of serious concern. But recently, the pendency of cases in the Supreme Court has shown a downward trend. The pendency of cases which was **1,04,936** as on **31st December, 1997** came down to **58,794** in 2004 and further down to **46,926** as on **31st Dec. 2007.**[26] As per latest available information, 57,179 cases were pending in the Supreme Court of India as on 30.6.11. The number has now increased to 63.843 as on May 2014.

Pendency in High Courts

The pendency of cases in the High Courts which was **33.65 lakh** as on **31st December, 1999** increased to **35,54,687 on 31st** December, 2001. The figures of pendency in the High Courts as on **31st December,** 2007 **is 37,00,223**. The number of cases pending in the High Courts were 42,17,903 as on 30.9.2010. Various measures have been adopted in the High Courts for expeditious disposal of cases including classification and grouping of cases, computerization of records in all the High Courts. But the result is not satisfactory because there are cases pending in Madhya Pradesh, Patna, Rajasthan and Calcutta High Court since 1950, 1951, 1955 and 1956 respectively.[27] As per a latest information, there are 4.4 million cases pending before the high courts as on December 2013.

Pendency of cases in Subordinate Courts

The situation of the pendency of cases is worst in the Subordinate Courts. As per available information, the pendency of cases in District/subordinate courts as on **31st December, 1997** was about **2 Crore**, then to **2.02 Crore** as on **21st December, 1998** and which has now increased to 2,5285,982 as on **31st December, 2007.**[28] As per December 2013, there are at least 27.6 million cases pending in subordinate courts while 4.4 million are pending in various high courts. Retired Delhi High Court judge Justice S.N. Dhingra said the government must "appoint more judges" to try the pending cases. Dhingra told IANS that such courts were established for "clearing the massive backlog in court cases on a priority basis".

While the maxim 'justice delayed is justice denied holds true in all such cases, it is important to know the reasons for the delay. Delay is mainly caused *inter alia* due to delay in investigation, delay in framing issues/charges, delay in trial, non-attendance of witnesses, absence of lawyers, witnesses turning hostile, repeated adjournment of cases, lack of accountability of judges, delay in appointment of judges and a host of other causes. It is, hence, the duty of the judiciary to enforce the rule of law and to guard against the erosion of the rule of law. While noting with surprise the attitude of judges, the **Supreme Court** in a case [29] observed: "*Our justice system has become so dehumanized that lawyers and judges don't feel a sense of revolt in caging people in jail for years*". The Court further said that justice should not only be done but should also appear to have been done. Similarly, whereas justice delayed is justice denied, justice withheld is even worse than that. The inordinate, unexplained and negligent delay in pronouncing the judgment is alleged to have actually negatived the right of appeal conferred upon the convicts under the provisions of the Code of Criminal Procedure.

Equal justice for all is a cardinal principle on which entire system of administration of justice is based. It is so deep-rooted in the body and spirit of common law as well as civil law jurisprudence that the very meaning which we attribute to the word 'justice' embraces it. The greatest challenge to the justice delivery system is the delay in the disposal of cases and prohibitive cost of litigation. Experience has shown that adjudication of disputes through Courts, while unavoidable, doesn't, in every case, provide a satisfactory or amicable solution.[30]

Alternative Dispute Resolution or ADR mechanisms have been evolved to present a solution to legal disputes and to do complete justice to the parties in conflict. It is a voluntary process which is gradually gaining legal recognition. ADR is, at present, a movement world-over to find an answer to never-ending litigation. The society as well as the parties to the dispute are equally under an obligation to resolve the dispute before it disturbs the peace in the family, business community, society or ultimately humanity as a whole. Arbitration, negotiation, mediation, conciliation and Lok Adalat are some of the accepted modes of alternative dispute resolution mechanisms.

Certain kinds of disputes such as matrimonial disputes, family disputes with neighbours and several other categories of petty civil and criminal cases, which form a substantial percentage of pending litigation, can be better and more satisfactorily resolved by organized and institutionalized processes of arbitration, mediation, conciliation or Lok Adalat through intervention of public-spirited and respected senior citizens.

Considering the mammoth size of areas, alternative modes of dispute settlement is the best way to reduce the number of cases filed everyday. The **Malimath Committee** made various recommendations on this aspect and a Bill to amend Civil Procedure Code was brought which contained *inter alia* provisions for making it obligatory for the court to refer the dispute after the issues are framed for settlement either by way of arbitration, conciliation, mediation, judicial settlement or through Lok Adalat.[31] It is only after parties fail to get their disputes settled through alternative dispute resolution methods that the suit shall proceed further in the Court in which it was filed. Besides this, there are other methods like setting up of Fast Track Courts, use of plea bargaining, widening the ambit of compoundable offences, decriminalization of petty offences, etc. by which arrears of cases can be reduced. It is expected that efforts of these kinds would definitely help to reduce the burden on the Courts and decrease the accumulation of arrears.

In a democratic society like India, for protecting and enhancing the rights of the people, the judiciary besides the Legislative and the executive body plays an important role. For the enforcement of rights of citizens and remedies thereto in case of violation thereof, Courts have been established at all levels in the country. These courts, by interpreting the laws, enhance justice to the individual and the society at large. With the rapid growth in the population and the development in industrial and technological fields, the work load of the judiciary has increased considerably. With the increase in workload, the efficiency of the courts is hampered badly.

With the increase in the rate of pending cases and declination of pronouncement of judgments, our society now truly considers that "Justice delayed is Justice denied". Due to the delay in rendering justice, people are losing faith in the judicial system. The mounting arrears of cases in the trial and appellate courts coupled with increased recourse to court cases on account of awareness of rights on the part of the citizens, various legislative enactments and administrative measures touching the lives of citizens at all levels, have assumed serious proportions.

Life and liberty of a citizen guaranteed under Art 21 includes life with dignity and liberty with dignity. Liberty must mean freedom from humiliation and indignities at the hands of the authorities to whom the custody of a person may pass temporarily or otherwise under the law of the land. A dignified life is not possible unless an accused is assured speedy disposal of his case. Therefore, speedy trial has been implied as a fundamental right under Art 21.

Individual liberty is a cherished right and perhaps one of the most valuable fundamental right guaranteed by our constitution. The interest of society can be served only if the Constitutional provisions are implemented in its strict sense and individual liberty of every person is harmonized with the social interest of the society. The state, as a guardian of the fundamental rights of its people, is duty-bound to ensure speedy trial and avoid any excessive delay in the trial of cases which could result in grave miscarriage of justice. It is in the interest of all concerned that the guilt or innocence of the accused is determined as quickly as possible. On pre-trial confinement, at times, an accused remains in jail for much longer period than even the maximum sentence which can be awarded to him on conviction for the offence of which he is accused. Many poor people, who fail to provide financial security and surety, have to remain in jail for years. Thus, our prisons are over-crowded resulting in heavy loss of state exchequers which could have been saved by speedy disposal of cases. It is, therefore, the bounden duty of the trial court to ascertain that the cases are disposed of speedily at least of the under-trials who are languishing in jails for years. Yet the judiciary is unable to enforce this, partly for want of adequate number of courts and Judges and partly due to their indifferent attitude towards the pending cases.

Criminal law remains ineffective without quick trial and prompt punishment. For a variety of reasons, witnesses tend to retract from their previous statements. Those won over by threats or inducement, turn hostile. Investigating officers and prosecutors loose heart; Judges feel helpless. People loose confidence in the judiciary as either criminals go scot-free or innocents continue to be harassed. Thus, delay in disposing cases amounts to punishing an accused before he is tried and guilt is proved. This cycle of vices is harmful for the development and peace of any civilized society.

All these above issues led us to take up the particular area wherein we will be making an effort to adumbrate the pros and cons of justice delivery system in India with a eye on 'right to speedy trial' which is implied under Art. 21 of the Indian constitution.

Notes and References

1. Report of Law Commission of India on Expeditious Investigation and Trial of Criminal Cases against Influential Public Personalities Report No. 239 Submitted to the Supreme Court of India in WP (C) NO. 341/2004, MARCH 2012, p. 4.
2. Data received from High Courts.
3. Table 4.9, Crimes in India, 2010 Statistics, published by National Crime Records Bureau, Ministry of Home Affairs, Government of India.
4. *Ibid.*, Table 4.13.
5. http://www.hindustantimes.com/india-news/justice-has-a-mountain-to-climb-of-31-3-million-pending-cases/article1-1259920.aspx, Ideation and written by : Sourjya Bhowmick Research : Shreya Chatterjee, Visualization : Vignesh Radhakrishnan, Source : Supreme Court and Parliamentary Q and A.
6. *Ibid.*, Tables 4.9 and 4.13.
7. *Ibid.*, Figures At A Glance - 2010.
8. *Ibid.*, Table 9.1.
9. *Ibid.*, Table 9.2.
10. *Ibid.*, Figures At A Glance - 2010.
11. *Ibid.*, Table 4.11.
12. Data received from High Court of Jharkhand.
13. See Transcript of Constituent Assembly, *supra* note 20.
14. See Lachmandas Kewalram Ahuja *v.* Bombay (1952) S.C.R. 710.
15. *Id.*
16. See e.g. Madhu Limaye *v.* Magistrate, (1971) 2 S.C.R. 711 (holding that undertrials may be detained in order to ensure that they appear in court for their eventual trial and where there may be a threat to community peace if they are released); Ranbir Singh Sehgal *v.* Punjab (1962) S.C.R. Supl. (1) 295 (noting that an undertrial prisoner is not necessarily exempt from being placed in solitary confinement, although the reasons for being held in solitary must not be arbitrary and must have a basis in law); Leo Roy Frey *v.* Superintendent, (1958) S.C.R. 822 (holding that a valid rebuttal to a defendant's claim of *habeus corpus* is for the prosecution simply to provide a "production of the order or warrant for the apprehension and detention of an undertrial"); Kanta Prashad *v.* Delhi Admin., (1958) S.C.R. 1218.
17. See e.g., Granville Austin, working A Democratic Constitution: The Indian Experience (1999); Upendra Baxi,The Indian Supreme Court and Politics (Eastern Book Co.) (1980);
   Rajeev Dhavan, The Supreme Court of India: A Socio-Legal Critique of its Juristic Techniques (1977); S.P. Sathe, Judicial Activism in India:

Transgressing Borders And Enforcing Limits (New Delhi: Oxford University Press) (2002); Krishnan, Scholarly Discourse, *supra* note 18.

18. See Sathe, *supra* note 56, at 106; Krishnan, Scholarly Discourse, *supra* note 18; see also Carl Baar, Social Action Litigation in India: The Operations and Limitations on the World's Most Active Judiciary, 19 POL'YSTUD. J. 140-50 (1990); Marc Galanter & Jayanth K. Krishnan, Bread for the Poor: Access to Justice and Rights of the Needy in India, 55 Hastingsl. J. 789, 795 (2005) [hereinafter Galanter & Krishnan, Bread for the Poor]; Jayanth K. Krishnan, Lawyering for a Cause and Experiences from Abroad, 94 CAL.L.R EV. 575 (2006) [hereinafter Krishnan, Lawyering for a Cause].
19. (1979) 3 S.C.R.169.
20. *Id.* Professor Upendra Baxi has written one of the most detailed and analytical account of this case. As Baxi notes, in reality there were several iterations of the decision, involving six different interim orders. (At the time of his writing, "the final orders in the writ petition... [were] yet to emerge"). For a comprehensive review of these various interim rulings, see Upendra Baxi, The Supreme Court Under Trial: Undertrials and the Supreme Court, 1 S.C.C. (JOUR.) 35, 35-51(1980). It is important to note that while Justice Bhagwati was a crusader for the undertrials in the Post-Emergency Era, he also was part of the majority in the infamous case (during the Emergency Rule) that allowed the government to wield unfettered powers, including the power to abrogate the constitution's right to life and *habeas corpus* provisions. See A.D.M. Jabalpur v. Shukla, A.I.R. 1976 S.C. 1207. We are grateful to Mr. Viplav Sharma for his insights on this important case.
21. See supratext accompanying note 59.
22. See Khatoon *v.* Home Ministry, (1979) 3 S.C.R. 169 (referencing the Sixth Amendment of the United States Constitution and the United States Bail Reform Act of 1966 as well as "[t]he experience of enlightened Bail Projects in the United States such as Manhattan Bail Project and D.C. Bail Project shows that even without monetary bail it has been possible to secure the presence of the accused at the trial in quite a large number of cases").
23. See Maneka Gandhi *v.* India, (1978) 2 S.C.R. 621.
24. *Id.* Again, for a complete treatment of this crucial ruling, see Sathe, *Supra* note 56.
25. (1980) 1 SCC 81.
26. Figure was given by Chief Justice K.G. Balakrishnan while inaugurating the "All India Seminer on Judicial Reform", held from 23rd-25th Feb. 2008 in New Delhi.
27. *Ibid.*
28. *Ibid.*
29. *Kadra Pahadiya* v. *State of Bihar* (1983) 2 SCC 104.
30. J.S. Verma; New Dimensions of Justice; 2nd ed., 2003; p. 145.
31. See S. 89, Civil Procedure Code (added by the amendment Act of 2002).

2

Right to Speedy Trial as a Part of Fundamental Human Rights in India

1. RIGHT TO SPEEDY TRIAL UNDER VARIOUS STATUTES IN INDIA

The quest for justice has been an idea which mankind has been aspiring for generations down the line. Our Constitution reflects this aspiration in the preamble itself. Among the noble aims and objectives of the Constitution, the founding fathers accorded the highest place to 'Justice'. The Preamble speaks of "We, the people of

India" resolve to secure *inter alia* "Justice–social, economic and political" to "all its citizens". The juxtaposition of the words and concepts in the Preamble is important. Most significantly, 'Justice' is placed higher than the other principles of 'Liberty', 'Equality' and 'Fraternity'. Again, the Preamble clearly enjoins precedence to social and economic justice over political justice. People turn to the judiciary in the quest of justice. Justice is thus a constitutional mandate. But justice that comes too late has no meaning at all to the person it is meant for. During a prolonged and unending trial, the priorities of an accused person towards his life change along with the circumstances. In cases where the accused is the head of a family and is the only bread earner, it is not only the accused but his family members also suffer because of delays in trial. Therefore, in order to decide the fate of lakhs of litigants, speedy trial should be recognized as an urgent need of the present judicial system. It will help to enhance the faith of the general public in the present judicial system. Keeping in mind the paramount importance of speedy trial, it is important to see as to how it has been dealt with under the Indian laws:

1.1 Under the Constitution of India

The Indian Constitution does not contain any express provision regarding the right to speedy trials. But the same is implied under **Article 21** of the Constitution. Article 21 provides that "no person shall be deprived of his life or personal liberty except according to procedure established by law". The most important terms in this provision are '*procedure established by law*". A procedure prescribed by law for depriving a person of his liberty cannot be termed as 'reasonable, fair and just' unless it ensures a speedy trial for determination of guilt of the accused. No procedure which doesn't ensure a reasonable quick trial be regarded as 'reasonable, fair and just' and will be in contravention of **Article 21 of the Constitution** and hence is not valid under law.[1] Breach of this fundamental right has the potential of making the entire prosecution liable to be quashed and closed and the accused in all such cases will have to be declared innocent and set free. Speedy trial is, hence, the essence of criminal trial and there can be no doubt that a delay in trial *per se* constitutes denial of justice.

Life and liberty of a citizen guaranteed under Article 21 includes life with dignity and liberty with dignity. Liberty must mean freedom from humiliation and indignities at the hands of whom the custody of a person may pass temporarily or otherwise, under the law of the land. Individual liberty is a cherished right and perhaps one of the most valuable fundamental rights guaranteed by our Constitution. If this right is violated or invaded upon, except strictly in accordance with law, the victim is entitled to apply to the Courts for immediate relief. The interest of society can be served only if the constitutional provisions are implemented in its strict sense and the individual liberty of every person is harmonized with the social interest of the society. The liberty of a person cannot be dealt with in any other manner by any of the state authorities. Such approaches do not advance true social interest. Continued indifference to such right is bound to erode the structures of our democratic society.[2]

The State as a guardian of the fundamental rights of its people is duty-bound to ensure speedy trial and avoid any excessive delay in trial of criminal cases that could result in grave miscarriage of justice. Speedy trial is in public interest as it serves societal interest also. It is in the interest of all concerned that the guilt or innocence of the accused is determined as early as possible.[3] Once an accused person is able to establish that this basic and fundamental right under Art. 21 has been violated, it is up to the State to justify that this infringement of fundamental right has not taken place, that the restrictions or provisions of law are reasonable and that the procedure followed in the case is not arbitrary but is just, fair, without delay, expeditious and reasonable. In case, the State fails to do so, the case made out against the accused person should be dropped and closed. In case of pre-trial confinement, sometimes the time which an accused person spends in jail is much more than even the maximum sentence, which can be awarded to him on conviction for the offence of which he is accused. Thus, our prisons are over-crowded which is causing heavy loss to our State exchequers. Crores of rupees can be saved by speedy disposal of cases of such under-trials. Many poor people are not able to provide financial securities as well as sureties and thus have to remain in jail even if the trial is delayed and prolonged. It is the bounded duty of the trial Courts to ascertain that the cases are disposed of speedily at least of the under-trials who are languishing in jail, yet the judiciary is unable to enforce this for want of adequate number of courts and judges.[4]

Further, the Constitution of India under **Article 22** imposes restriction on the detention of any person by the police beyond 24 hours without the authority of a magistrate. It provides that every person who is arrested and detained should be produced before the nearest judicial magistrate within a period of 24 hours of such arrest, excluding the time necessary for the journey from the place of arrest to the court of the magistrate and no such person shall be detained in custody beyond the said period without the authority of a magistrate.[5] This article thus seeks to prevent illegal detention of people and ensure a prompt action on the part of the police.

1.2 Under the Criminal Procedure Code

The regime of criminal trial in India is regulated by the Code of Criminal Procedure (hereinafter referred to as Cr.P.C) and the Indian Penal Code (IPC). The procedure for criminal trial as provided in the Cr.P.C lays down a number of provisions aimed at reducing the delay in the investigation and trial of offences. The constitutional guarantee of speedy trial emanating from Article 21 is well reflected in the various provisions of the code.

Personal liberty being the corner-stone of our social structure, the provisions pertaining to trial of a person accused of an offence has special significance and importance. So for ensuring speedy disposal of a case, the pre-trial procedure should be reasonably fast. So every police officer or other person arresting any person without warrant **shall forthwith** communicate to him full particulars of the offence for which he is arrested or other grounds for such arrest.[6] Timely information of the grounds of arrest enables him to move proper Courts for bail or to make expeditious arrangements for his defence.

Section 56 of Cr.P.C provides that a police officer making an arrest without warrant shall, **without unnecessary delay** and subject to the provisions regarding bail, take or send the person arrested before a Magistrate having jurisdiction in the case or before the officer in charge of a police station, but the police officer or other person executing a warrant of arrest shall (subject to the provisions of S. 71 as to security) without unnecessary delay bring the person arrested before the court in which he is required by law to produce such person, provided that such delay shall not, in any case, exceed twenty-four hours exclusive of the time necessary for the journey from the place of arrest to the Magistrate's Court.[7]

According to **Section 57 of Cr. P.C.**, no police officer shall detain in custody a person arrested without warrant for a longer period than, under all circumstances of the case is reasonable and such period shall not, in the absence of a special order of a Magistrate under S.167, exceed twenty-four hours excluding the time necessary for the journey from the place of arrest to the court of the magistrate. **Section 157 of Cr.P.C** requires the officer-in-charge of a police station to send forthwith the report of the commission of an offence to the concerned magistrate.

Section 167 of Cr.P.C. provides that whenever any person is arrested and detained in custody and it appears that the investigation cannot be completed within the period of twenty-four hours fixed by S. 57 and there are grounds for believing that the accusation or the information is well-founded, the officer in charge of the police station or the police officer making the investigation (not below the rank of the sub-inspector), shall forthwith transmit to the nearest Judicial Magistrate a copy of the entries made in his diary relating to the case and shall at the same time forward the accused to such magistrate.[8] Such magistrate, whether he has or has not the jurisdiction to try the case, from time to time, may authorize the detention of the accused in such custody for a term **not exceeding fifteen days** as a whole; and if he has no jurisdiction to try the case or commit it for trial and considers further detention as unnecessary, he may order the accused to be forwarded to a Magistrate having jurisdiction.[9] The magistrate, who has jurisdiction to try the case, may authorize the detention of the accused person, otherwise than in the custody of the police, beyond the period of fifteen days if he is satisfied that adequate grounds exits for doing so but even the magistrate cannot authorize the detention of the accused person in custody for a total period exceeding:

(i) **Ninety days**, where the investigation relates to an offence punishable with death, imprisonment for life or imprisonment for a term of not less than ten years; and

(ii) **Sixty days**, where the investigation relates to any other offence.[10]

If in a case triable by a magistrate as a summons case, the investigation is not concluded within six months from the date on which the accused person was arrested, the magistrate is required to stop further investigation into the offence. The investigation is allowed to go on beyond six months only if the investigating officer satisfies the magistrate that for special reasons and in the interest of justice the continuation of the investigation is necessary.[11]

Sec. 173 (1) of Cr. P.C. requires the police officer to complete the investigation **"without unnecessary delay"** and forward the report to the magistrate "as soon as the investigation is completed". Further **Sec. 207** requires that a copy of documents like the police report, first information report (F.I.R.), statements recorded **U/s 161(3)** (except those portions for which request for exclusion is made) confessions and statements **U/s 164** or any other documents or relevant extract thereof is to be given free of cost to the accused **"without delay"**.[12] **Sec. 208** requires that where, in a case instituted otherwise than on a police report, it appears to the Magistrate issuing process under **Sec. 204** that the offence is triable by the court of session, the Magistrate shall **without delay** furnish to the accused, free of cost, a copy of statements and confession, if any, recorded under section 200, 202, 161, 164 or any documents produced before the magistrate on which the prosecution proposes to rely.

All the abovementioned provisions of Cr. P.C. pertain to the stage of investigation into an offence. These provisions, besides laying down in broad terms certain limits subject to which investigation is to be carried out, also put limits upon detention pending investigation. **Section 468 Cr. P.C.** also in a way impose a time limit for completion of investigation as it debars courts from taking cognizance of certain minor offences after the expiry of certain period of limitation.[13] **Section 469** marks that the period of limitation commences from the date of the offence; or where the commission of the offence was not known to the person aggrieved by the offence or to any police officer, the first day on which such offence comes to the knowledge of aggrieved person or to any police officer, whichever is earlier; or where it not known by whom the offence was committed, the first day on which the identity of the offender is known to the person aggrieved by the offence or to the police officer making the investigation into the offence, whichever is earlier.[14]

Section 309 of Cr. P.C. mandates expeditious conduct of trial. In particular, it requires that when the examination of witnesses has once begun, the same shall be continued from day-to-day until all the witnesses in attendance have been examined, unless the court finds the adjournment of the proceeding beyond the following day to be necessary for reasons to be recorded. Though the Code recognizes power of the court to adjourn the proceedings from time to time after the cognizance of the offence is taken or after commencement of the trial after recording reason for doing so, yet it provides that when the witnesses are present in the court, no adjournment or postponement shall be granted, without examining them, except for special reasons to be recorded in writing.[15] No adjournment is to be granted for the purpose only of enabling the accused person to show cause against the sentence proposed to be imposed on him. Further the terms on which an adjournment or postponement may be granted included, in appropriate cases, the payment of costs by the prosecution or the accused.[16]

Any party to a proceeding may, as soon as may be, after the close of his evidence, address concise oral arguments, and may, before he concludes the oral arguments, if any, submit a memorandum to the court setting forth concisely the arguments in support of his case.[17] No adjournment of the proceeding shall be granted for the purpose of filing the written arguments unless the court, for reasons to be recorded in writing, considers it necessary to grant such adjournments.[18] The court may, if it is of the opinion that the oral arguments are not concise or relevant, regulate such arguments.

Section 437(6) of the code provides that if the trial of a person accused of a non-bailable offence is not concluded within a period of **sixty days** from the date fixed for taking evidence, such person is to be released on bail if he is in custody.

In addition to these provisions, there is another provision which aims at achieving the same end of expeditious conduct of trial which is **Section 353**. This Section provides that the judgment shall be pronounced in open court by the presiding officer **immediately after the termination of the trial** or at some subsequent time of which notice shall be given to the parties or their pleaders.[19] Thus, the provision clearly requires the judgment to be pronounced soon after the completion of the trial so that there is no delay in the pronouncement of the same.

The perusal of these provisions enshrined in the Criminal Procedure Code thus indicates that the code has given due importance to the speedy completion of criminal trials so that the constitutional guarantee of providing speedy justice to the people can be achieved in its realistic sense.

1.3 Under Civil Procedure Code

The Code of Civil Procedure is the basic Code of Procedure governing civil actions in our country. There are many provisions in the Code of Civil Procedure dealing with speedy disposal of cases. These provisions are as follows:

Order XVII of the **Code of Civil Procedure** provides that the Court may, if sufficient cause is shown, at any stage of the suit, grant time to the parties or to any of them and may, from time to time adjourn the hearing of the suit for reasons to be recorded in writing:

> Provided that no such adjournment shall be granted more than three times to a party during hearing of the suits.[20]

In every such case, the court shall fix a day for further hearing of the suit and shall make such orders as to costs occasioned by the adjournment or such higher costs as the court deems fit:[21]

Provided that—

(a) When the hearing of the suit has commenced, it shall be continued from day-to-day until all the witnesses in attendance have been examined, unless the court finds that for exceptional reasons to be recorded by it, the adjournment of the hearing beyond the following day is necessary.

(b) No adjournment shall be granted at the request of a party, except where the circumstances are beyond the control of that party.

(c) The fact that pleader of a party is engaged in another court, shall not be a ground for adjournment.

(d) Where the illness of a pleader or his inability to conduct the case for any reason, other than his being engaged in another court, is put forward as a ground for adjournment, the court shall not grant adjournment unless it is satisfied that the party applying for adjournment couldn't have engaged another pleader in time.

(e) Where a witness is present in court but a party or his pleader is not present or the party or his pleader, though present in court, is not ready to examine or cross-examine the witness, the court may, if it thinks fit, record the statement of the witness and pass such orders as it thinks fit dispensing with the examination-in-chief or cross-examination of the witness, as the case may be, by the party or his pleader not present or not ready as aforesaid.[22]

Besides this, there is **Section 89** of the Code of Civil Procedure which deals with settlement of disputes outside the Court. **Sec. 89(1)** provides that where it appears to the court that there exist elements of a settlement which may be acceptable to the parties, the Court shall formulate the terms of settlement and give them to the parties for their observations and on receiving the observations of the parties, the Court may formulate the terms of possible settlement and refer the same for—

(a) Arbitration;
(b) Conciliation;
(c) Judicial settlement including settlement through Lok Adalat; and
(d) Mediation.

Where a dispute has been referred—

(a) for arbitration or conciliation, the provisions of the Arbitration and Conciliation Act, 1996 shall apply as if the proceedings for arbitration or conciliation were referred for settlement under the provisions of that Act;
(b) to Lok Adalat, the Court shall refer the same to the Lok Adalat in accordance with the provisions of Section 20(1) of the Legal Services Authorities Act, 1987 and all other provisions of that Act shall apply in respect of the dispute referred to the Lok Adalat;
(c) for judicial settlement, the Court shall refer the same to a suitable institution or person and such institution or person shall be deemed to be a Lok Adalat and all the provisions of the Legal Services Authorities Act, 1987 shall apply as if the dispute were referred to a Lok Adalat under the provisions of that Act; and
(d) for mediation, the Court shall effect a compromise between the parties and shall follow such procedure as may be prescribed.[23]

Order XX, Rule 1 of the **Civil Procedure Code** provides that the Court, after the case has been heard, shall pronounce the judgment in open court, either at once or as soon thereafter as may be practicable and when the judgment is to be pronounced on some future day, the court shall fix a day for that purpose, of which due notice shall be given to the parties or their pleaders.

When the judgment is not pronounced at once, every endeavour shall be made by the court to pronounce the judgment within thirty days from the date on which the hearing of the case was concluded but, where it is not practicable so to do on the ground of the exceptional and extraordinary circumstances of the case, the court shall fix a future day for the pronouncement of the judgment and such day shall not ordinarily be a day beyond sixty days from the date on which the hearing of the case was concluded and due notice of the day so fixed shall be given to the parties or their pleaders.[24] Before the Amendment Act of 1976, no time limit was provided between the hearing of the arguments and the delivery of the judgment. There was a persistent demand all over the country for imposing a time limit for the delivery of a judgment after the conclusion of hearing of a case. Even the Supreme Court had to observe in the case of *R.C. Sharma* v. *Union of India*:

> "The Civil Procedure Code doesn't provide a time limit for the period between the hearing of the arguments and the delivery of a judgment. Nevertheless, we think that an unreasonable delay between the hearing of the arguments and the delivery of a judgment, unless explained by exceptional or extraordinary circumstances, is highly undesirable even when written arguments are submitted. It is not unlikely that some points which the litigant considers important may have escaped notice. But, what is more important is that litigants must have complete confidence in the results of litigation. This confidence tends to be shaken if there is excessive delay between the hearing of the arguments and the delivery of a judgment. *Justice, as we have often observed, must not only be done but must manifestly appear to be done.*"

(emphasis supplied)

There is a provision in the Code of Civil Procedure **under Order VI** having in some way the object of reducing delay in the trial of a case. It provides that the court may at any stage of the proceedings allow either party to alter or amend his pleadings in such manner and on such terms as may be just or all such amendments shall be made as may be necessary for the purpose of determining the real questions in controversy between the parties.[25] By way of amendment, a rider has been imposed on the amendment of pleadings which provides that no application for amendment shall be allowed after the trial has commenced, unless the court comes to the conclusion that inspite of diligence, the party could not have raised the matter before the commenced of trial.[26] So, now the parties cannot apply for amendment of their pleadings after the commencement of trial which is very important for expeditious proceedings of a case. The object of the provision *inter alia* is to reduce delay in the final disposal of cases.

Order XVIII, Rule (3A) of the **Code of Civil Procedure** provides that any party may address oral arguments in a case, and shall, before he concludes the oral arguments, if any, submit if the Court so permits concisely and under distinct headings written arguments in support of his case to the Court and such written arguments shall form part of the record. A copy of such written arguments shall be simultaneously furnished to the opposite party. **No adjournment shall be granted** for the purpose of filing the written arguments unless the Court, for reasons to be recorded in writing, considers it necessary to grant such adjournment.[27] The Court shall fix such time-limit for the oral arguments by either of the parties in a case, as it thinks fit.[28]

Order VIII of the **Code of Civil Procedure** also provides a provision for speedy progress of trial by way of giving a time-limit for filing written statement. It provides that the defendant shall, **within 30 days** from the date of service of summons on him, present a written statement of his defence :

> Provided that where the defendant fails to file the written statement within the said period of thirty days, he shall be allowed to file the same on such other day, as may be specified by the Court, for reasons to be recorded in writing, but which shall not be later than ninety days from the date of service of summons.[29] Under this Rule, there is a legislative mandate that written statement of defence is to be filed within 30 days. However, if there is a failure to file such written statement within stipulated time, the court can at the most extend further period of 60 days and no more. Under the Act, the legislative

intent is not to give 90 days of time but only maximum 30 days for filing the version by the opposite party. Therefore, the aforesaid mandate is required to be strictly adhered to

Section 35B of the **Code of Civil Procedure** provides that if, on any date fixed for the hearing of a suit or for taking any step therein, a party to the suit fails to take the step which he was required by or under this code to take on that date, or obtains an adjournment for taking such step or for producing evidence or on any other ground, the court may, for reasons to be recorded, make an order requiring such party to pay to the other party such costs as would, in the opinion of the court, be reasonably sufficient to reimburse the other party in respect of the expenses incurred by him in attending the court on that date payment of such costs, on the date next following the date of such order, shall be a condition precedent to the further prosecution of—

(a) the suit by the plaintiff, where the plaintiff was ordered to pay such costs,

(b) the defence by the defendant, where the defendant was order to pay such costs.[30] The very object behind this provision is to ensure the attendance of the plaintiff or the defendant, as the case may be, on the scheduled date and to make them punctual regarding other schedule of the case on the fear of being penalised, so that the case may be decided within a reasonable time. Therefore, this provision is inserted to put a check upon the delaying tactics of litigating parties.

So from the above provisions of the Civil Procedure Code, it can safely be said that provisions of the Code are clear enough to indicate that there should not be undue delay in the disposal of cases.

2. SPEEDY TRIAL IN SOME OTHER COUNTRIES

2.1 Speedy Trial in USA

The right to a speedy trial finds expression in the U.S. Constitution, State constitutions, State and Federal statutory laws, and the State and federal case laws. The Sixth Amendment to the U.S. Constitution, and the case law surrounding this amendment, provide the best place to start analysis of the basic questions of primary concern: What interests does this right protect? When and why are these interests triggered? And how should these interests be protected, both to prevent their violation whenever possible and to remedy the effects of violations when violations nonetheless occur? The words of the Sixth Amendment, *inter alia* guarantee that **"In all criminal prosecutions, the accused shall enjoy the right to a speedy and public trial by an impartial jury....."**[31]

This Bill of Rights, originally applied only against the federal government. It has since been "incorporated" via the **Fourteenth Amendment** to apply to the states as well (*Klopfer* v. *North Carolina*)[32]. In a nutshell, the framers designed the right to protect a person from prolonged *de facto* punishment—extended accusations that limit his liberty and besmirch his good name before he had a full and fair chance to defend himself. If government accuses someone, it must give him the right speedily so that he can clear himself at the trial and regain his good name and full liberty. And if government holds the accused in extended pre-trial detention, Courts must ensure that the accuracy of the trial itself will not thereby be undermined as might occur if a defendant's prolonged detention itself causes the loss of key exculpatory evidence.

The United State of America is the only country which has enacted a legislation to implement the constitutional guarantee of speedy trial to all accused persons. The Act is known as the **Speedy Trial Act** which was passed in **1974**. This Act prescribes a set of time limit for carrying out major events in criminal proceedings. This Act requires the trial of a defendant should commence **within 70 days** from the date of filing of the indictment or from the date on which the defendant appears before a judicial officer of the Court, whichever is later. The indictment must be filed **within 30 days** from the date of arrest or service of summons. If a violation of the provisions of the Speedy Trial Act occurs, the indictment against the defendant must be dismissed. The District Court, however, retains the discretion to dismiss the indictment either with or without prejudice. In the case of *United States* v. *Taylor,*[33] the question was of determining whether a dismissal of an indictment for non-compliance with the Speedy Trial Act should be with or without prejudice. The Court observed that the District Court must at least consider the seriousness of the offence, the facts and circumstances of the cases, which can lead to the dismissal and the impact of a re-prosecution on the administration of the Speedy Trial Act as well as on the administration of justice.

So, in determining whether to dismiss with or without prejudice, a district court "shall consider, among others, each of the following factors:[34]

- The seriousness of the offense;
- The facts and circumstances of the case which led to the dismissal; and
- And the impact of a re-prosecution on the administration of justice."

A district court is not required to dismiss an indictment with prejudice for every violation of the Speedy Trial Act. The decision whether to dismiss a complaint under the Speedy Trial Act with or without prejudice is entrusted to the sound discretion of the District Judge and no preference is accorded to either kind of dismissal. Although not as harsh a sanction as dismissal with prejudice, dismissal without prejudice is meaningful because it, *inter alia*, forces the Government to obtain a new indictment if it decides to re-prosecute as well as exposes the prosecution to dismissal on the ground of law of limitation.[35]

The right to a speedy trial is not only an important safeguard to prevent undue and oppressive incarceration but it serves to minimize anxiety and concern that accompany the accusation. This right helps to limit the possibility of impairing the ability of an accused person to defend himself. This right was actuated in the recent past and the courts have laid down a series of decisions opening up new vistas of fundamental rights. In fact, more cases are coming up before the Courts for quashing of proceedings on the ground of inordinate and undue delay stating that the invocation of this right even need not await formal indictment of charge.[36]

As the guarantee of a speedy trial is one of the most basic rights preserved by the Constitution of USA, the protection afforded by this guarantee is activated only when a criminal prosecution has begun and extends only to those persons who have been accused in the course of that prosecution. Invocation of the right need not await indictment, information or other formal charge but begins with the actual restraints imposed by arrest if those restraints precede the formal preferring of charges.

Moreover, in order to ensure that accused persons are not rushed to trial without an adequate opportunity to prepare their cases, the Congress amended the Act in 1979 to provide a minimum time period during which trial must commence. The amended Act provides that trial may not begin less than 30 days from the date the defendant first appears in court, unless the defendant agrees in writing to an earlier date. In *United States* v. *Rojas Contreras*[37] the U.S. Supreme Court held that this 30-day trial preparation period is not restarted upon the filing of a substantially similar superseding indictment. If the indictment is dismissed at the defendant's request, the provisions of the Act apply afresh upon reinstatement of the charge. If the indictment is dismissed at the request of the government, the 70-days time begins to run again upon the filing of the second indictment. If trial ends in a mistrial or the court grants a motion for a new trial, the second trial must begin within 70 days from the date the decision of retrial becomes final.

Certain pre-trial delays are automatically excluded from the Act's time limits, such as delays caused by pre-trial motions. In *Henderson* v. *United States*,[38] the Supreme Court held that the Act excludes "all time between the filing of a motion and the conclusion of the hearing on that motion, whether or not a delay in holding that hearing is reasonably necessary." Other delays excluded from the Act's time limits include: delays caused by the unavailability of the defendant or an essential witness; delays attributable to a co-defendant; and delays attributable to the defendant's involvement in other proceedings, including delay resulting from an interlocutory appeal. In *United States* v. *MacDonald*,[39] the Court held that the speedy trial clause was not implicated by the action of the United States when, in May 1970, it proceeded with a charge of murder against defendant under military law but dismissed the charge in October of that year, and he was discharged in December. In June of 1972, the investigation was reopened but the grand jury was not convened until August of 1974, and MacDonald was not indicted until January of 1975. The period between dismissal of the first charge and the later indictment had none of the characteristics, which called for application of the speedy trial clause. The period between arrest and indictment must be considered in evaluating a speedy trial claim. *MacDonald Case* was applied in *United States* v. *Loud Hawk*[40] by holding that the speedy trial guarantee was inapplicable to the period during which the government appealed for dismissal of an indictment, since during that time the suspect had not been subject to bail or otherwise restrained. Further there was no denial of speedy trial since prosecution's position on appeal was strong, and there was no showing of bad faith or dilatory purpose. If the interlocutory appeal is taken by the defendant, he must "bear the heavy burden of showing an unreasonable delay caused by the prosecution or wholly unjustifiable delay by the appellate court" in order to win dismissal on speedy trial grounds.

The right of a speedy trial is necessarily relative. It is consistent with delays and depends upon circumstances. It secures a right to a defendant. It does not preclude the rights of public justice. No length of time is *per se* too long to pass scrutiny under this guarantee, but on the other hand, neither does the defendant have to show actual prejudice caused by delay. The Court rather has adopted an *ad hoc* balancing approach. "We can do little more than identify some of the factors which courts should assess in determining whether a particular defendant has been deprived of his right. Though some might express them in different ways, we identify four such factors: Length of delay, the reason for the delay, the defendant's assertion of his right, and prejudice to the defendant. The fact of delay triggers an inquiry and is dependent on the circumstances of each case. Reasons for the delay will vary. A deliberate delay for advantage will weigh heavily, whereas the absence of a witness would justify an appropriate delay, and such factors as crowded dockets and negligence will fall between these other factors. Delays caused by the prosecution's interlocutory appeal will be judged by the above factors, of which the second one, that is, 'the reason for the appeal' is the most important.

A defendant may not expressly waive his rights under the Speedy Trial Act. This was ruled in *Untied States* v. *Saltzman.*[41] However, if the trial judge determines that "ends of justice" served by a continuance of the trial outweigh the interest of the public and the defendant in a speedy trial, delay occasioned by such continuance is excluded from the Act's time limits. The judge must set forth, orally or in writing, his reasons for granting the continuance. The government should never rely on a defendant's unilateral waiver of his rights under the Act. It is the duty of the prosecution to bring a defendant to trial, and the failure of the defendant to demand the right is not to be construed as a waiver of the right; yet, the defendant's acquiescence in delay when it works to his advantage should be considered against his later assertion that he was denied the guarantee, and the defendant's responsibility for the delay would be conclusive. Finally, a court should look to the possible prejudices and disadvantages suffered by a defendant during a delay. While the accused/defendant cannot unilaterally waive his rights under the Speedy Trial Act, he can forfeit his right to obtain a dismissal of the case for a claimed violation of the Act by failing to move for dismissal prior to trial. The statute provides that failure of the defendant to move for dismissal prior to trial shall constitute a waiver of the right to dismissal under this section.[42]

A series of cases decided by the Supreme Court during the second half of the twentieth century laid down **seven general propositions** concerning the constitutional right to a speedy trial:

(1) The Court has repeatedly identified three major and distinct interests protected by the Sixth Amendment speedy trial clause: an interest in avoiding prolonged pretrial detention, an interest in minimizing the anxiety and loss of reputation accompanying formal public accusation, and an interest in assuring the ultimate fairness of a delayed trial.

(2) The Court has made clear that the major evils of pre-trial restraints on liberty and loss of reputation occasioned by accusation exist quite apart from the third major evil of possible prejudice to an accused's defence at trial.

(3) The Court has held that the clause simply does not apply to the time between the commission of the crime and the time that the defendant is in some way "accused" (usually by arrest or indictment) by the government. In other words, the clause applies only to the formal "accusation period"—the period between governmental accusation and trial.

(4) Relatedly, the Court has held that the clause does not apply to any period during which the government drops its initial charges while retaining the right to re-indict later. In such a case the defendant is not "accused" during this time, and so the speedy trial clock stops ticking against the government during this period.

(5) The Court has held that if pre-accusation delay compromises the defendant's ability to defend himself or

herself, the main safeguard against injustice comes from the applicable statute of limitations. In cases of substantial prejudice to a fair trial caused by a prosecutor's purely strategic delay in bringing the initial accusation, defendants may also seek relief by appealing to general due process principles.

(6) The Court has said that the judicial remedy for speedy trial violations of dismissing the case with prejudice that is, dismissing with no possibility of refilling charges later is unsatisfactorily severe because it means that a defendant who may be guilty of a serious crime will go free, without ever having been tried. Such a remedy, the Court has noted, is more severe than the Fourth Amendment exclusionary rule, which limits the introduction of certain evidence, but typically does not altogether bar a trial.

(7) Nonetheless, the Court has repeatedly held that dismissal with prejudice is the only possible remedy for speedy trial clause violations. Given the first six propositions, the analytic soundness of proposition seven seems questionable to some scholars, although the law appears quite clear on this point.[43]

It may be seen that the first of these seven principles set out above suggests that each of the three interests protected by the clause may have a different time limit. Imagine, for simplicity, a case in which the liberty interest would be violated by anything more than a month of pretrial detention: by hypothesis, any detention longer than this would be an unacceptable deprivation of liberty for a man who has yet to receive all the safeguards of a full-blown trial-a man who has not yet been, and may never be, convicted of anything. Now imagine a second defendant, charged with the identical crime but released on her own recognizance pending trial. In this second case, no pre-trial detention interest exists, and her distinct anxiety and reputation interest would not necessarily be violated by a similar one-month gap between indictment and trial. For example, a full year might elapse before this distinct constitutional interest, which demands that at some point an accused person must be allowed to answer the government's accusation and thereby clear her good name, would be violated. The fair trial interest may have a different time period depending on the particular ways in which the government's accusation threatens to impede a defendant's ability to fully defend himself or herself at trial. For example, some pre-trial detentions might severely obstruct the defendant's ability to assemble evidence and witnesses for his trial defence; other detentions might not, depending on the particular conditions of confinement and state of evidence; and still other indictments will not involve any pre-trial detention.

Moreover, it is clear that the clause is violated by long detention regardless of what happens later on but an impermissibly lengthy detention violates the clause whether it ends in a trial or in the charges being dropped. So far as the pre-trial liberty interest is concerned, it is the detention, and not the trial, that violates the speedy trial clause. This is suggested by the second proposition: the pre-trial liberty and reputation interests are independent of the conditions of the trial, as the Court made clear in 1971 in the case of *United States* v. *Marion*, [44] *Marion case* also illustrated the third proposition in upholding an indictment handed down three years after prosecutors supposedly knew about the crime and defendants' involvement in it. The Court said that the defendants were simply not "accused" during those three years. In accordance with the fifth proposition, the Court ruled that the statute of limitations was the defendants' primary safeguard, and further noted that if defendants could show substantial prejudice to their defence created by a bad-faith prosecutor seeking delay simply to gain tactical advantage, a due process challenge would be appropriate.

Although the Constitution speaks of a speedy trial as the right of the 'accused', the Court has recognized that society at large also has its own legitimate interests in the prompt resolution of criminal accusations. Many defendants, especially guilty defendants, might prefer to delay their trials, perhaps in the hope that prosecutorial evidence will become stale, making it more difficult for the government to carry its ultimate burden of proof beyond reasonable doubt. But the Constitution does not give the defendant a general right to an 'unspeedy' trial unlike, for example, the Sixth Amendment right of counsel, which is accompanied by a general right not to have counsel. Nevertheless, at some extreme point, an accusation period could be so short as to violate general due process principles, so a defendant must be given sufficient time to arrange his defense, as the Supreme Court recognized in its famous ruling in *Powell* v. *Alabama*.[45]

In the light of analysis of the nature and timing of speedy trial clause rights, it remains to ponder how these rights should be legally protected and remedied. Although the Court has said that dismissal with prejudice is the only possible remedy, there are reasons to doubt the analytical soundness of this assertion. Consider the first interest protected by this clause, the bodily liberty interest offended by overlong pretrial detention. Judges can simply refuse to allow this violation to happen by issuing writs of *habeas corpus* directing the release of prisoners who have served as much pre-trial time in jail as the clause will tolerate. Historically, the speedy trial right in England tightly intertwined with the famous **English Habeas Corpus Act of 1679**. However, *habeas* is less of a remedy than a means of prevention. What should the remedy be when the judge fails to issue a writ? One controversial possibility would be to allow for compensatory and punitive damages directly against the government. Extending its landmark ruling in *Bivens* v. *Six Unknown Agents of the Federal Bureau of Narcotics*,[46] which held that government officials who conducted unreasonable searches could be sued directly under the Fourth Amendment, the Court could find a direct cause of action against the government itself under the Sixth Amendment's speedy trial clause. Indeed, unconstitutionally long detentions would seem to be a subset of unreasonable seizures of persons, and so the Fourth Amendment might seem directly applicable as well. The prospects for such a doctrinal development, however, seem bleak. The most natural damage remedy would lie against the government itself. (Judges who ordered the detention would enjoy judicial immunity; prosecutors who allowed the defendant to languish in jail before the trial begins would likewise claim that a court had authorized the detention; and the jailor would insist that he was acting in good faith relying upon a judicial order of confinement.) But principles of sovereign immunity would most likely make it difficult to prevail in a damage suit brought directly against the government, even though its executive and judicial agents combined to deprive a defendant of his constitutional rights to bodily liberty.

Similarly, for the second speedy trial interest i.e. reputation, the judge can prevent violations by simply quashing indictments that linger too long, with permission to re-indict whenever the prosecutor is ready to proceed immediately to trial. Again, if the judge fails to prevent a violation, civil damages would be a remedial possibility, just as they are in other cases of damaged reputation (e.g., slander and libel) where the accused may be charged by the government of having committed an infamous act, but has been denied his right to speedily clear his name in a fair trial. Here, too, the problem of sovereign immunity has blocked the development of this analytically attractive remedy.

One of the main virtues of damage remedies is that they seek to vindicate the rights of innocent men and women wrongly detained and accused; dismissal with prejudice is not a true or tailored remedy for someone who is clearly innocent, and would have obviously prevailed at the trial. In other words, although dismissal with prejudice might well vindicate whatever fair trial interest might exist, it does nothing to redress the analytically distinct wrongs of pre-trial loss of bodily liberty and reputation that can occur when a defendant is held too long in pre-trial detention, or accused too long without a chance to speedily clear his name at trial. The framers of the Constitution cared a great deal about innocent persons, and designed many provisions in the Fourth, Fifth, and Sixth Amendments to protect these innocent persons from erroneous punishments and impositions. The speedy trial clause is clearly, at its core, designed to give an innocent man, who is wrongly accused, a right to a speedy trial so that he can clear his good name. These two major interests, i.e. interest in reputation and liberty is ill-served by the current absence of good remedies to make innocent men and women suffer when these interests have been violated by government.

Consider finally the fair trial interest, designed to ensure that an overlong accusation itself (which of course may trigger pre-trial detention and which may cause an immediate loss of reputation that worsens with every day the indictment lingers) does not compromise the ability of a defendant to put on a full and unimpaired defence at the trial. Here too, the Amendment is centrally designed to protect an innocent defendant from being erroneously imposed upon. A judge could again prevent violations of this interest by ordering the pre-trial release of the defendant or ordering the conditions of confinement softened so that the confinement does not cause the loss of key exculpatory evidence. If this fails, however, there are several possible judicial remedies. One is dismissal with prejudice. The idea here is simple: if, because of the government's unconstitutionally long accusation period, a fair trial is simply no longer possible, then the trial itself should be permanently aborted, and the defendant set free. This is a precisely tailored remedy but only for that subset of cases in which the fair trial interest has been incurably compromised. Another possible option, in cases where it is less than clear that a trial would itself be unfair, is to rely on the due process rule of in *re Winship*[47], requiring the government to prove guilt beyond a reasonable doubt in criminal cases. A defence argument to the jury that an unreasonable delay by the prosecutor's office caused key evidence to be lost could certainly be a ground for reasonable doubt.

Defendants in criminal cases, under the Sixth Amendment, have the right to a speedy trial. In the case of *Barker* v. *Wingo*[48] the U.S. Supreme Court laid down a four-part *ad hoc* balancing test for determining whether the defendant's speedy trial right has been violated:

1. *Length of delay*: A delay of a year or more from the date on which the speedy trial right "attaches" (the date of arrest or indictment, whichever occurs first) was termed "presumptively prejudicial", but the Court has never explicitly ruled that any absolute time limit applies.
2. *Reason for the delay*: The prosecution may not excessively delay the trial for its own advantage, but a trial may be delayed to secure the presence of an absent witness or other practical considerations.
3. *Time and manner in which the defendant has asserted his right*: If a defendant acquiesces to the delay when it works to his own benefit, he cannot later claim that he has been unduly delayed.
4. Degree of prejudice to the defendant which the delay has caused.

If the reviewing court finds that a defendant's right to a speedy trial was violated, then the indictment must be dismissed and/or the conviction overturned. The Supreme Court has held that, since the delayed trial itself is the state action which violates the defendant's rights, no other remedy would be appropriate. Thus, a reversal or dismissal of a criminal case on speedy trial grounds means that no further prosecution for the alleged offence can take place.

Right to Public Trial

The Court has ruled that the right to a public trial as guaranteed by the Sixth Amendment is not absolute. In cases where excess publicity would serve to undermine the defendant's right to due process, limitations can be put on public access to the proceedings. Trials are often closed at the behest of the government with claims that there is "an overriding interest based on findings that closure is essential to preserve higher values and is narrowly tailored to serve that interest."

Right to a Jury

The right to a jury has always depended on the nature of the offence with which the defendant is charged. Petty offences, that is, those punishable by imprisonment for not more than six months are not covered by the jury requirement. Even where multiple petty offences are concerned, where the total time of imprisonment possibly exceeding six months, the right to a jury trial does not exist.

Originally, the Supreme Court held that the Sixth Amendment's right to a jury trial indicated a right to "a trial by jury as understood and applied at common law, and includes all the essential elements as they were recognized in this country and England when the Constitution was adopted." Therefore, it was held that juries had to be composed of twelve persons and that verdicts had to be unanimous, as was customary in England. When, under the Fourteenth Amendment, the Supreme Court extended the right to a trial by jury to defendants in state courts, it re-examined some of the standards. It has been held that the twelve came to be the number of jurors by "historical accident", and that a jury of six would be sufficient but anything less would deprive the defendant of a right to trial by jury. Although on the basis of history and precedent the Sixth Amendment mandates unanimity in a federal jury trial, the Supreme Court has ruled that the 'Due Process Clause' of the Fourteenth Amendment, while requiring States to provide jury trials for serious crimes, does not incorporate all the elements of a jury trial within the meaning of the Sixth Amendment and does not require jury unanimity.

Another factor in determining the impartiality of the jury is the nature of the panel from which the jurors are selected. Panel must represent a fair cross-section of the community; the defendant may establish that the requirement was violated by showing that the allegedly excluded group is a "distinctive" one in the community or that the representation of such a group in the panel is unreasonable and unfair in regard to the number of persons belonging to such a group and that the under-representation is caused by a systematic exclusion in the selection process. Thus, in *Taylor* v. *Loussianna*,[49] the Supreme Court invalidated a state law that exempted women who had not made a declaration of willingness to serve in the jury, while not doing the same for men.

The Constitution originally required that defendants be tried by juries selected from the state in which the crime was committed. The Sixth Amendment extends the rule by requiring trials to occur in districts ascertained by statute. As the Supreme Court found in *Beavers* v. *Henkel*[50] the place where the offence is charged to have occurred determines the trial's location. Where multiple districts are alleged to have been locations of the crime, any of them may be chosen for the trial. In cases of offences not committed in any state (for example, offences committed at sea), the place of trial may be determined by Congress.

Right to Notice of Accusation

A defendant has, under the Sixth Amendment, the right to be informed of the nature and cause of the accusation against him. Therefore, an indictment must allege all the ingredients of the crime to such a degree of precision that it would allow the accused to assert double jeopardy if the same charges are brought up in subsequent prosecution. The Supreme Court held in *United States* v. *Carll*[51] that "in an indictment it is not sufficient to set forth the offence in the words of the statute, unless those words of themselves fully, directly, and expressly, without any uncertainty or ambiguity, set forth all the elements necessary to constitute the offence intended to be punished." Vague wording, even if taken directly from a statute, does not suffice. However, the government is not required to hand over written copies of the indictment free of charge.

Right to Confrontation

The defence, under the Sixth Amendment, must have an opportunity to "confront" and cross-examine the witnesses. The confrontation clause relates to the common law rule preventing the admission of hearsay, that is to say, testimony by one witness as to the statements and observations of a person for the purpose of proving that the statement or observation was accurate. Certain exceptions to the hearsay rule have been permitted; for instance, admissions by the defendant are admissible, as are dying declarations. Nevertheless, the Supreme Court has held that the hearsay rule is not exactly the same as the confrontation clause: Hearsay may, in some circumstances, be admitted though it is not covered by one of the long-recognized exceptions; for example, prior testimony may sometimes be admitted if the witness is unavailable. Yet in *Cawford* v. *Washington*[52] the Supreme Court increased the scope of the confrontation clause in the trials. Justice Scalia's opinion made any "testimonial" out-of-court statements inadmissible if the accused did not have the opportunity to cross-examine that accuser. "Testimonial" becomes a term of art here, meaning any statements that an objectively reasonable person in the declarant's situation would have deemed likely to be used in court. The most common application of this would come after a declarant made a statement to a police officer, and then that officer testifies about that statement at the trial.

The defendant must also be permitted to call witnesses in his favor. If such witnesses refuse to attend, they may be compelled to do so by the court at the request of the defendant. In some cases, however, the court may refuse to permit a defence witness to testify. If, for example, a defence lawyer fails to notify the prosecution of the identity of its witnesses in order to gain a tactical advantage, the witnesses whose identities were undisclosed may be precluded from testifying.

The right to confront and cross-examine witnesses also applies to physical evidence; the prosecution must present physical evidence to the jury, providing the defence ample opportunity to cross-examine its validity and meaning. Prosecution generally may not refer to evidence without first presenting it.

Right to Counsel

The Sixth Amendment guarantees the Right to counsel of defendants to procure the assistance of counsel. The defendant has the right not only to be heard through such attorneys as he pleases but furthermore, the defendant may represent himself. The court may, however, deny the defendant such a right when it is deemed that the defendant is incompetent to waive the right to counsel.

Originally, the clause was not interpreted as requiring the state to appoint counsel where the defendant could not afford to do so. The Supreme Court began to expand the interpretation of the clause in *Powel* v. *Alabama*[53] in which it held, "in a capital case, where the defendant is unable to employ counsel, and is incapable adequately of making his own defence because of ignorance, feeble mindedness, illiteracy, or the like, it is the duty of the court, whether requested or not, to assign counsel for him." In *Jhonson* v. *Zerbst*[54], the Supreme Court ruled that in all federal cases, counsel would have to be appointed for defendants who were too poor to hire their own. When deciding *Betts* v. *Baddy*[55] the Court declined to extend this requirement to the state courts under the Fourteenth Amendment unless the defendant demonstrated "special circumstances" requiring the assistance of counsel.

In 1960, the Court extended the rule that applied in federal courts to state courts. It held in *Hamilton* v. *Alabama*[56] that counsel had to be provided at no expense to defendants in capital cases when they so requested, even if there was no "ignorance, feeble mindedness, illiteracy, or the like as stated in *Brewer* v. *Williams*[57] the rights granted by Sixth and Fourteenth Amendments "mean at least that a person is entitled to the help of a lawyer at or after the time that judicial proceedings have been initiated against him, whether by formal charge, preliminary hearing, indictment, information, or arraignment." Once adversaries proceeding have begun against a defendant, he has a right to legal representation when the government interrogates him

Right to Self-representation

In *Faretta* v. *California*[58], the Supreme Court has expounded the right to represent yourself by holding that the power to choose or waive counsel lies with the accused, and the state can not intrude, though it later held in *Godinez* v. *Moran*,[59] that the state could deny the waiver if it believed the accused less than fully competent to adequately proceed without counsel. The Supreme Court also held in *Bounds* v. *Smith*[60], that the constitutional right of "meaningful access to the courts" can be satisfied by counsel *or* access to legal materials.

2.2 Speedy Trial in England

In England, the right of the accused to expeditious trial found its first expression in the **Habeas Corpus Act, 1679**. **Section 6** of the Act provided for release on bail or discharge of persons detained on accusation of high treason or felony in the Courts of Assizes or Sessions, if indictment could not take place in the second term after committal. **Assizes Act, 1889** and **Magistrate's Court's Act, 1952** limit pre-conviction custody of the accused. Some steps to regulate and limit the actual duration of the prosecution process was made in the **Crown Court Rules, 1982** and **Indictment Rules, 1983** which are statutory regulations. Under these rules, the bill of indictment is to be prepared **within 28 days of committal** and the trial is to commence **within 8 weeks of committal**. Both these limits may be extended by the court.

Section 22 of the **Prosecution of Offender's Act, 1985** enables the Secretary of State to prescribe custodial and overall time limit, in respect of preliminary stages of trial. "Preliminary Stage" means proceedings prior to indictment, and in summary trials, proceeding prior to taking of evidence for the prosecution. The actual time limit has to be prescribed by the Secretary of State through delegated legislation. The consequence of non-adherence to overall time limits is acquittal. According to the provisions now in force, the maximum period of custody between the accused's first appearance and the commencement of the summary trial is **56 days**. While in case of offences triable on indictment exclusively, the maximum period of custody between the accused's first appearance and the time when the court decides whether or not to commit the accused to the Crown Court for trial is **70 days**.

The Privy Council, while dealing with the question of delay in trial expressly affirmed the principles laid down by the Supreme Court of the America in *Barker* v. *Wingo*[61]. In *Bell* v. *Director of Prosecution*, *Jamica*,[62] the Privy Council expressed the desirability of applying the same criteria as laid down in *Barker* v. *Wingo* to any constitution, written or unwritten, which protects an accused from oppression by delay in criminal proceedings.

3. JUDICIAL PRONOUNCEMENTS

The Indian Judiciary plays a very pivotal role in the dispensation of justice by providing fair and just trial to all its citizens. There are various pronouncements of the Supreme Court and the High Courts on the subject of speedy trial wherein the Courts have questioned the delays and set aside the following prosecution and discharged the accused. The Court's concern about the problem of delay in trial finds reflection in these judgments.

In *State of West Bengal* v. *Anwar Ali Sarkar*,[63] a Bench of seven judges of the S.C. held that "the necessity of a speedy trial is too vague and uncertain to form the basis of valid and reasonable classification. It is too indefinite as there can hardly be any definite objective test to determine it. It is no classification at all in the real sense of the term as it is not based on any characteristics which are peculiar to persons or to cases which are to be subjected to the special procedure prescribed by the Act".

In *Machander* v. *State of Hyderabad*,[64] the Supreme Court refused to remand the case back to the trial court for fresh trial because of delay of five years between the commission of the offence and the final judgment of the Supreme Court. The Supreme Court observed:

> "We are not prepared to keep persons on trial for their live and under indefinite suspense because trial judges omit to do their duty .... We have to draw a nice balance between conflicting rights and duties .... While it is incumbent on us to see that the guilty do not escape, it is even more necessary to see that the person accused of crimes are not indefinitely harassed .... While every reasonable latitude must be given to those concerned with the detection of crime and entrusted with administration of justice, but limits must be placed on the lengths to which they may go."

In *Chajoo Ram* v. *Radhey Shayam*[65] delay in trial was one of the factors on the basis of which the Supreme Court dropped the further proceedings.

In *State of Uttar Pradesh* v. *Kapil Deo Shukla*[66] though the court found the acquittal of the accused unsustainable, it refused to order a remand or direct a trial after a lapse of 20 years.

The Supreme Court in *Maneka Gandhi* v. *Union of India*[67] held that Article 21 of the Constitution of India confers a fundamental right on every individual not to be deprived of his life or personal liberty except according to procedure established by law and such procedure as required under Article 21 has to be "fair, just and reasonable" and not "arbitrary, fanciful or oppressive".

In *Charles Sobharaj* v. *Suptd., Central Jail, Tihar*,[68] Krishna Iyer observed:

> "Whenever Fundamental rights are flouted or Legislative protection ignored, to any prisoner's prejudice, this court's writ will run, breaking through stone walls and iron walls, to right

the wrong and restore the rule of law. Then the parrot cry of discipline will not deter security, will not scare discretion, and will not dissuade the judicial process".

The Apex Court's decision in *Hussainara Khatoon (iv)* v. *Home Secretary, State of Bihar*[69] is a land mark one in the development of speedy trial jurisprudence. A writ of *habeas corpus* was filed on behalf of men and women languishing in jails in the state of Bihar awaiting trial. Some of them had been in jail for a period much beyond what they would have spent had maximum sentence been imposed on them for the offence of which they were accused. Alarmed by the shocking revelations made in the writ petition and concerned about the denial of the basic human rights to those "victims of callousness of the legal and judicial system", Supreme Court went on to give a new direction to the Constitutional jurisprudence. In doing so, the court heavily relied on its decision in an earlier case in which the court gave a very progressive interpretation to Article 21 of the Constitution. Taking this interpretation to its logical end, Bhagwati J., in *Hussainara Khatoon's case* said:

> "...Procedure prescribed by law for depriving a person of his liberty cannot be reasonable, fair or just unless that procedure ensures a speedy trial for determination of the guilt of such person. No procedure which does not ensure a reasonably quick trial can be regarded as 'reasonable, fair or just' and it would fall foul of Article 21. There can, therefore, be no doubt that speedy trial, and by speedy trial we mean reasonably expeditious trial, is an integral and essential part of the fundamental right to life and liberty enshrined in Article 21."

Bhagwati J. also added that the state cannot be permitted to deny the constitutional right to speedy trial on the ground that the state has no adequate financial resources to incur the necessary expenditure needed for improving the administrative and judicial machinery with a view to ensuring speedy trial. As far as the question of consequences of violation of the right to speedy trial is concerned, it was raised but left unanswered by the court.

The law laid down in *Hussainara Khatoon's case* was followed in a number of subsequent decisions of the Supreme Court. In *State of Bihar* v. *Uma Shankar Ketriwal*[70] the High Court quashed the proceedings on the ground that the prosecution which commenced

16 years ago and still in progress, is an abuse of the process of the court and should not be allowed to go further. Refusing to interfere with the decision of the High Court in the appeal, the Supreme Court said with regard to the delay that such protraction itself means considerable harassment to the accused and that there has to be a limit to the period for which criminal litigation is allowed to go on at the trial stage.

The Court again considered the applicability of the right to speedy trial in *State of Maharashtra* v. *Champalal Punjaji Shah*[71] and observed that while deciding the question whether there has been a denial of the right to a speedy trial, the court is entitled to take into consideration whether the delay was unintentional, caused by over-crowding of the court's docket or under-staffing of the prosecutors and whether the accused contributed a fair part to the time taken. This decision was severely criticized by **Prof. Upendra Bakshi,** [72] who said that even if the accused prefers interlocutory appeals it cannot be inferred that he contributed to delay, as by doing so he merely avails the opportunity-structure provided by the law of the land. Moreover, legal strategies are determined by the accused person's counsel and not by the accused himself as he cannot be expected to understand subtleties of law and its procedures. He further added that delay caused by failure on the part of the courts to assign priority to the organization of day-to-day work cannot be said to be unintentional.

In *Kadra Pahadiya* v. *State of Bihar* [73] the Supreme Court by following the principle of *Hussainara Khatoon case* observed that :

> "..... any accused who is denied this right of speedy trial is entitled to approach this Court for the purpose of enforcing such right and this court in discharge of its constitutional obligation has the power to give necessary directions to the state governments and other appropriate authorities for securing this right to the accused".

In this case several undertrials were languishing in jail for 8 years without their trial having made any progress. The Apex court commented:

> *"It is crying shame upon our adjudicatory system which keeps men in jail for years on and without trial".*[74]

In *Raghubir Singh* v. *State of Bihar* [75] a Bench of two judges of the Supreme Court held that the right to speedy trial is one of the dimensions of the fundamental right to life and liberty guaranteed by Art. 21. The question whether the right to speedy trial has been infringed depends upon various factors. A host of question may arise for consideration: Was there delay? Was the delay inevitable having regard to the nature of the case? Was the delay unreasonable? Was the delay caused by the tactics of the defence? There may be other questions as well. But ultimately the question of infringement of the right to speedy justice is one of fairness in the administration of criminal justice even as 'acting fairly' is the essence of the principle of natural justice and "a fair and reasonable procedure" is what is contemplated by the expression "procedure established by law" in Art. 21.

In *Madhu Mehta* v. *Union of India*,[76] the Supreme Court held that "Art. 21 is relevant in all stages. Speedy trial in criminal cases, though may not be a fundamental right, is implicit in the broad sweep and content of Art. 21. Speedy trial is part of one's fundamental right to life and personal liberty".

In *T.V. Vatheeswaran* v. *State Tamil Nadu*[77] the Court again reiterated the significance of the right to speedy trial. In this case, the accused persons were acquitted by the trial court whereupon an appeal was filed before the High Court which allowed it after a period of six years and remanded the case for retrial. Reversing the decision of the High Court, the Supreme Court held that the pendency of criminal appeal for six years before the High Court is itself a regrettable feature of this case and a fresh trial nearly seven years after the alleged incident is bound to result in harassment and abuse of judicial process.

The Supreme Court in *Sheela Barse* v. *Union of India*[78] addressed the question left unanswered in *Hussainara Khatoon's case* and dealt specifically with the procedure to be followed in matters where accused was less than 16 years of age. The court held that where a juvenile is accused of an offence punishable with imprisonment of 7 years or less, investigation was to be completed within 3 months of the filing of F.I.R. or else the case was to be closed. Further, all proceedings in respect of the matter had to be completed within further six months of filing of the charge-sheet. The S.C observed:

"The right to speedy trial is a right implicit in Article 21 of the Constitution and the consequence of violation of this right could be that the prosecution itself would be liable to be quashed on the ground that it is in breach of the fundamental right".

In *Rakesh Saxena* v. *State through C.B.I.*[79] the court quashed the proceedings on the ground that any further continuance of the prosecution after lapse of more than six years is uncalled for.

In *Srinivas Pal* v. *Union Territory of Arunachal Pradesh*,[80] the court quashed the proceedings against the accused on the ground of delay in investigation and commencement of trial. In this case, the investigation commenced in Nov. 1976 and the case was registered on completion of the investigation in Sept. 1977. Cognizance was taken by the Court in March 1986.These facts were held sufficient to quash the proceedings particularly when the offence charged was a minor one namely, section 304A read with Section 338 of IPC.

In *Madhav Rao Jivaji Rao Scindia* v. *Sambhaji Rao Chandroji Rao*,[81] the S.C. observed that the Court cannot be utilized for any oblique purposes and where in the opinion of the Court, chances of an ultimate conviction are bleak and therefore, no useful purpose is likely to be served by allowing criminal prosecution to continue, the Court may quash the proceedings.

In *T.J. Stephen* v. *Parle Bottling Co. (P) Ltd.*,[82] the court disallowed recommencement of the prosecution after a lapse of twenty years on the ground that it would not be in the interest of justice.

The Supreme Court in *Diwan Naubat Rai* v. *State through Delhi Administration*[83] refused to quash the proceedings as it found that the accused himself was mainly responsible for delay of which he was complaining.

In *State of A.P.* v. *R.V. Pavithran*[84] the Supreme Court upheld the decision of the High Court in quashing the F.I.R. on the ground of inordinate delay in completing the investigation. The court further observed that while examining the plea of delay in completing the investigation, the court should have regard to all the relevant circumstances and that it is not possible to formulate any inflexible guidelines or rigid principles of uniform application for speedy investigation nor is it possible to stipulate any arbitrary period of limitation for completing the investigation.

In *Mihir Kumar* v. *State of West Bengal*[85] where a criminal proceeding had been pending for 15 years from the date of the offence, the Supreme Court held that it amounted to violation of the constitutional right to speedy trial of a 'fair, just and reasonable' procedure, hence the accused was entitled to be set free.

The Supreme Court in *Abdul Rahman Antulay* v. *R.S. Nayak*,[86] gave a landmark decision and finally adjudicated upon the questions left open in *Hussainara Khatoon's case*[87], like the scope of the right, the circumstances in which it could be invoked, its consequences and limits, etc. The salient features of the decision are as follows:

(a) Right to speedy trial flowing from Article 21 encompasses all the stages namely, the stage of investigation, inquiry, trial, appeal, revision and retrial.
(b) In every case, where right to speedy trial is alleged to have been infringed, the first question to be put and answered is who is responsible for the delay? Proceedings taken by either party in good faith, to vindicate their rights and interests, as perceived by them, cannot be taken as delaying tactic nor can the time taken in pursuing such proceedings be counted towards delay.
(c) While determining whether undue delay has occurred one must have regard to all the circumstances, including nature of offence, number of accused and witnesses, the workload of the court concerned, prevailing local conditions and so on.
(d) Each and every delay does not necessarily prejudice the accused. However, inordinately long delay may be taken as presumptive proof of prejudice. Prosecution should not be allowed to become a persecution. But when does the prosecution become persecution, depends upon the facts of a given case.
(e) Accused's plea of denial of speedy trial cannot be defeated by saying that the accused didn't demand a speedy trial.
(f) The Court has to balance and weigh the several relevant factors—'balancing test' and 'balancing processes—and determine in each case whether the right to speedy trial has been denied in a given case.
(g) Charge or conviction is to be quashed if the court comes to the conclusion that right to speedy trial of an accused

has been infringed. But this is not the only course open; it is open to the court to make such other appropriate order—including an order to conclude the trial within a fixed time where the trial is not concluded or the sentence where the trial has concluded, as may be deemed just and equitable in the circumstances of the case.

(h) It is neither advisable nor practicable to fix any time limit for trial of offences because time required to complete trial of a case depends on the nature of the case.

(i) An objection based on denial of right to speedy trial and for relief on that account should first be addressed to the High Court. Even if the High Court entertains such a plea, ordinarily it should not stay the proceedings, except in a case of grave and exceptional nature. Such proceedings in High Court must be disposed of on a priority basis.

The Supreme Court has emphasized the above propositions again and again. In *Kartar Singh* v. *State of Punjab*,[88] the Supreme Court has observed:

> "*The concept of speedy trial is read into Article 21 as essential part of the Fundamental Right to Life and Liberty guaranteed and preserved in our Constitution. This right to speedy trial begins with the actual restraint imposed by arrest and consequent incarceration and continues at all the stages of investigation, enquiry, trial, appeal and revision so that any possible prejudice that may result from impermissible and avoidable delay from the time of the commission of the offence till it consummates into a finality, can be averred*".

In *Santosh De* v. *Arachana Guha*[89] the Supreme Court quashed the prosecution on the ground of inordinate delay as the trial for corruption of a government servant was kept pending for 14 years.

In *Union of India* v. *Ashok K. Mehta*,[90] there was delay in trial but it was not attributable only to the prosecution and the respondent himself had contributed to the delay. Refusing to quash the prosecution in the instant case, the Court observed that the respondent could not be allowed to take advantage of his own wrong and take shelter under speedy trial to escape from prosecution

The guidelines laid down in *Antulay's case*[91] were adhered to in a number of cases which came to be considered by the Court subsequently. But a different note was struck in *"Common Cause" a registered society through its Director* v. *Union of India.*[92] In this case, the court directed release of under-trials on bail if the trial is going on for a certain period and the accused has been in prison for a certain period of time.

The Supreme Court has stated in *Common Cause Case*[93] said that even persons accused of minor offences have to wait for their trials for long periods. If they are poor and helpless, they languish in jails as there is no one to bail them out. The very pendency of criminal proceedings for long periods by itself operates as an engine of oppression. Accordingly, to protect and effectuate the right to life and liberty of the citizens guaranteed by **Article 21**, the Court issued certain general directions for releasing the under-trials on bail or personal bonds where trials had been pending for one year or more.

These directions are as follows:

(i) Where the offence under IPC or any other law for the time being in force for which the accused are charged before any Criminal Court are punishable with imprisonment not exceeding three years with or without fine and if the trial for such offences are pending for one year or more and the accused concerned haven't been released on bail but are in jail for a period of six month or more, the Court shall release such accused on bail or on personal bond to be executed by the accused on such conditions as may be found necessary.

(ii) Where the offence under IPC or any other law for the time being in force for which the accused are charged before any Criminal Court are punishable with imprisonment not exceeding five years with or without fine and if the trial for such offences are pending for two years or more and the accused concerned haven't been released on bail but are in jail for a period of six month or more, the Court shall release such accused on bail or on personal bond to be executed by the accused and subject to such conditions as may be found necessary.

(iii) Where the offence under IPC or any other law for the time being in force for which the accused are charged before any Criminal Court are punishable with imprisonment not exceeding seven years with or without fine and if the trial for such offences are pending for two years or more and the accused concerned haven't been released on bail but are in jail for a period of six months or more, the Court shall release such accused on bail or on personal bond to be executed by the accused and subject to such conditions as may be suitable in the light of Sec. 437, Cr.P.C

(iv) Where criminal proceedings are pending regarding traffic offences in any criminal Court for more than two years on account of non-serving of Summons to the accused or for any other reason whatsoever, the Court may discharge the accused and close the case.

(v) Where the cases pending in Criminal courts for more than two years under IPC or any other law for the time being in force are compoundable with the permission of the Court and if in such a case trials have still not commenced, the Criminal Court shall, after hearing the public Prosecutor and other parties or their representatives before it, discharge or acquit the accused, as the case may be, and close the case.

It also directed acquittal or discharge of an accused where for an offence punishable with imprisonment for a certain period, the trial had not begun even after a lapse of the whole or 2/3rd of the period. But the court excluded certain economic and other offences from the application of these guidelines. In a subsequent case, the Supreme Court clarified its order in *Common Cause Case*[94] and excluded from its application those cases where the pendency of criminal proceedings was wholly or partly attributable to the dilatory tactics adopted by the accused or on account of any other action on the part of the accused which resulted in prolonging the trial. The court also explained the expressions, "pendency of trial" and "non-commencement of trial".

In *R.D. Upadhyay* v. *State of Andhra Pradesh*[95] the Court gave directions with respect to the under-trials languishing in Tihar jail. Directions were given for nomination of special judges for disposing of the cases of murder. These cases were directed to be disposed of within a period of six months. The Court also gave directions for release of under-trials on bail.

In *M.V. Chauhan* v. *State of Gujarat*[96] a government employee was prosecuted and convicted on certain charges of corruption. The prosecution started in 1985 on the basis of the events which occurred in 1983. In an appeal against the conviction in 1997, the Supreme Court found that the sanction given by the government for this prosecution was invalid. The Court barred initiation of fresh prosecution against the appellant. The SC observed:

> "*Normally when the sanction order is held to be bad, the case is remitted back to the authority for reconsideration of the matter and to pass a fresh order of sanction in accordance with law. But, in the instant case, the incident is of 1983 and, therefore, after a lapse of fourteen years, it will not, in our opinion, be fair and just to direct that the proceedings may again be initiated from the stage of sanction so as to expose the appellant to another innings of litigation and keep him on trial for an indefinitely long period contrary to the mandate of Article 21 of the Constitution which, as part of Right to Life, philosophizes early end of criminal proceedings through a speedy Trial.*"

Another attempt was made to concretize the right to speedy trial in *Raj Deo Sharma* v. *State of Bihar.*[97] In this case, the Court directed closure of prosecution evidence on completion of **two years** in cases of offences punishable with imprisonment for period **not exceeding 7 years** and on completion of **3 years** in cases of offences punishable with imprisonment for period exceeding 7 years. But again the effect of this judgment was whittled down in the subsequent clarification order. In the clarification order it was laid down that the following periods could be excluded from the limit prescribed for completion of prosecution evidence in *Raj Deo Sharma's case*[98]:

(a) Period of pendency of appeal or revision against interim orders, if any, preferred by the accused to protract the trial;
(b) Period of absence of presiding officer in the trial court; and
(c) Period of three months, in case the office of public prosecutor falls vacant (for any reason other than expiry of tenure).

In *Rajiv Gupta* v. *State of Himachal Pradesh*[99] the S.C held that it is clear that if the trial of a case for an offence which is punishable with imprisonment up to three years has been pending for more than two years and if the trial is not commenced, then the criminal court is required to discharge and acquit the accused.

In *Anil Rai* v. *State of Bihar*[100] the Supreme Court observed that the justice should not only be done but should also appear to have been done. Similarly, whereas justice delayed is justice denied, justice withheld is even worse than that.

In *Akhtari Bi* v. *State of Madhva Pradesh*,[101] the Court held that if an appeal is not disposed of within a period of five years, for no fault of the convicts, such convicts may be released on bail on such conditions as may be deemed fit and proper by the Court.

In *All India Judges' Association* v. *Union of India*[102] the S.C. held that it is a constitutional obligation of the Supreme Court to ensure that the backlog of cases is decreased and efforts are made to increase the disposal of cases. Apart from the steps which may be necessary for increasing the efficiency of the judicial officers, it appears that the time has come for protecting one of the pillars of the Constitution, namely, the judicial system, by directing increase in the judges strength from the existing ratio of judge-population ratio.

In *N.S. Sahni* v. *Union of India*,[103] it was held that the right of an accused to have a speedy trial is now recognized as a right under Art.21. The procedural fairness required by Art. 21 including the right to speedy trial has, therefore, to be observed throughout and to be born in mind.

In *Usha Mahajan w/o Roshan Lal* v. *State*,[104] the petitioner was in jail for the last four and half years. The court held that the case of an accused in the judicial custody is not in the same pedestals as those enlarged on bail. Keeping accused in jail without trial not augur well for criminal justice delivery system. Therefore, the court gave direction for the day-to-day basis trial of the case.

In *Ahmad Ilahi* v. *State*[105] it was held that in view of the lingering and procrastinated proceedings it is directed that the learned trial court shall record the remaining evidence on day-to-day basis and decide the question of framing of charges positively within one month, failing which the proceeding against the petitioner shall stand quashed as no Court can be taken for a ride.

In *Durga Datta Sharma* v. *State*,[106] the prosecution under the Prevention of Corruption Act has not commenced after a period of 25 years. No charges had been framed and chances of commencing and concluding the trial in near future were not strong. Observing that the accused persons had already suffered a lot both mentally and physically during the last 25 years, the Court dropped all charges against the accused.

The Supreme Court on August 13, 2008 came down heavily on the delay in the disposal of the *Uphaar Fire Tragedy Case*. In this case, 59 persons were charred to death in a fire in Uphaar Cinema Hall during the screening of a Hindi Film 'Border' on the fateful night of June 13, 1997. A District Court in Delhi took 10 long years in Concluding the trial and thereafter the victims approached the Delhi High Court for speedy conclusion of the trial. On Nov. 20, 2007, the District Court convicted all 12 accused including Theature owner Sushil and Gopal Ansal, who were given sentences varying from 2 to 7 years. Then the accused appealed to the Delhi H.C. against the Conviction. On August 13, 2008, the victims again approached the Supreme Court for speedy disposal of the appeal. The Counsels of the victims pointed out to a Bench of Justice B.N. Agarwal and Justice G.S. Singhvi that while the trial concluded after 10 years following a lot of delay, there are now active attempts on the part of the accused to delay the disposal of the appeal before the High Court. The Bench not to miss an opportunity to call a spade said: "*The trial of the case took 10 years. It cannot be treated as an ordinary case. There is a clear evidence of criminal negligence*".

In the famous *BMW Case* which has been decided in September 2008 one BMW car mowed down six people in the early morning hours. The accused in this case was 22 years old, Sanjeev Nanda, grandson of former Naval Chief S.M. Nanda. The two key prosecution witnesses subsequently changed their version and said that they saw a truck, and not a BMW hitting the victims. But the Supreme Court finally sentenced the accused to five years imprisonment.

4. CONCLUSION

To sum up the discussion, it can be said that although the Constitution of India does not directly talk of the right to speedy trial but the same has been given a status of fundamental right by way of innovative interpretation of Art. 21 of the Constitution. Besides the Constitution, the Code of Criminal Procedure and the Code of Civil Procedure also guarantee the right to speedy trial in its various provisions. But above all, it is the judiciary which is instrumental in giving this right the status of fundamental right so that the Constitutional guarantee of providing speedy justice to the people can be achieved in its realistic sense.

Notes and References

1. *Hussainara Khatoon (IV)* V. *Home Secretary, State of Bihar,* AIR 1979 SC 1369.
2. B.K. Arora; *Law of Speedy Trial in India*; (2nd edition) 2005; p. 71.
3. *Ibid.*
4. *Supra* note 2, at p. 78.
5. Art. 22(2), The Constitution of India.
6. S. 50(1), The Code of Criminal Procedure, 1973.
7. S. 76, The Code of Criminal Procedure, 1973.
8. S. 167(1), The Code of Criminal Procedure, 1973.
9. S. 167(2), The Code of Criminal Procedure, 1973.
10. Proviso to S. 167(2), The Code of Criminal Procedure, 1973.
11. S. 167(5), The Code of Criminal Procedure, 1973.
12. S. 207 of the Code of Criminal Procedure provides that in any case where the proceeding has been instituted on a police report, the Magistrate shall without delay furnish to the accused, free of cost, a copy of each of the following:
    (i) the police report;
    (ii) the first information report recorded under S. 154;
    (iii) the statement recorded under S. 161(3) of all persons whom the prosecution proposes to examine as its witnesses, excluding the circumstances mentioned in S. 173(6);
    (iv) the confessions and statements, if any, recorded under S.164; and
    (v) any other document or relevant extract thereof forwarded to the Magistrate with the police report under S. 173(5).
13. S. 468 of the Code of Criminal Procedure provides that except as otherwise provided in this Code, no Court shall, after the expiry of the period of limitation, take cognizance of an offence which shall be—
    (a) six months, if the offence is punishable with fine only;
    (b) one year, if the offence is punishable with imprisonment for a term not exceeding one year; and
    (c) three years, if the offence is punishable with imprisonment for a term exceeding one year but not exceeding three year.
14. S. 369(1), The Code of Criminal Procedure, 1973.
15. S. 309(1), The Code of Criminal Procedure, 1973.
16. S. 309(2), Proviso, The Code of Criminal Procedure, 1973.
17. S. 314(1), The Code of Criminal Procedure, 1973.
18. S. 314(2), The Code of Criminal Procedure, 1973.
19. S. 353(1) of the Code of Criminal Procedure provides that the judgment in

every trial in any Criminal Court of original jurisdiction shall be pronounced in open Court by the presiding officer immediately after the termination of the trial or at some subsequent time of which notice shall be given to the parties or their pleaders—

(a) by delivering the whole of the judgment;
(b) by reading out the whole of the judgment; or
(c) by reading out the operative part of the judgment and explaining the substance of the judgment in a language which is understood by the accused or his pleader.

20. Order XVII, Rule-1, The Code of Civil Procedure
21. Order XVII, Rule 2, The Code of Civil Procedure
22. Order XVII, Rule 2, Proviso, The Code of Civil Procedure.
23. S. 89, The Code of Civil Procedure.
24. Order XX, rule-1, Proviso The Code of Civil Procedure (added by the Amendment Act of 1976).
25. Order VI, Rule-17, The Code of Civil Procedure.
26. Rule-17, Proviso(added by the amendment of the Code of Civil Procedure in 2002).
27. Order XVIII, Rule 3C, The Code of Civil Procedure.
28. Order XVIII, Rule 3D, The Code of Civil Procedure.
29. Order VIII, Rule-1, The Code of Civil Procedure.
30. Subsec. (1), Sec. 35B, The Code of Civil Procedure.
31. *Supra* Note-2 at p. 256.
32. 386 US 213 (1967).
33. 487 US 326(1988).
34. *Id* at p. 328.
35. *Id* at p. 329.
36. Supra note-26 at p 257.
37. 474 US 231 (1985).
38. 476 US 321 (330) (1986).
39. 456 US 1 (1982).
40. 474 US 302(1986).
41. 984 F.2d 1087.
42. *Id* at p. 986.
43. Supra Note- 31at p. 265.
44. 404 US 307 327.
45. 287 US 45 (1932).
46. 403 US 388 (1971).
47. 397 US 358 (1970).
48. 33 L Ed 2d 101.
49. 419 US 522 (1975).
50. 194 US 73 (1904).
51. 105 US 611 (1881).
52. 541 US 36 (2004).
53. 287 US 45 (1932).

54. 287 US 45 (1932).
55. 316 US 455 (1942).
56. 422 US 806 (1975).
57. 430 US 387 (1977).
58. 368 US 52 (1961).
59. 509 US 389 (1993).
60. 430 US 817 (1977).
61. 33 L Ed 2d 101.
62. (1985) 2 All ER 585.
63. AIR 1952 SC 75.
64. AIR 1955 SC 792.
65. AIR 1971 SC 1367.
66. (1972) 3 SCC 504.
67. (1978) 1 SCC 248.
68. (1979) I.S.C.R 514-15.
69. (1980) 1 SCC 81.
70. (1981) 1 SCC 85.
71. (1981) 3 SCC 610.
72. Upendra Bakshi; "*Right to Speedy Trial: Geese, Gender And Judicial Sauce*"; 2nd ed. 1986; p. 243.
73. (1983)2 SCC 104.
74. *Ibid.*
75. (1986) 4 SCC 481 : AIR 1987 SC 149 : 1986 SCC (Cri) 511.
76. (1989) 4 SCC 62 : AIR 1989 SC 2299: 1989 SCC (Cri) 705.
77. (1983) 2 SCC 68.
78. (1986) 3 SCC 632.
79. (1986) 3 SCC 505.
80. (1988) 4 SCC 36.
81. AIR 1988 SC 709.
82. 1988 Supp SCC 458.
83. (1989) 1 SCC 297.
84. (1990) 2 SCC 3440.
85. 1990 Cr LJ 26 (Cal).
86. (1992) 1 SCC 225.
87. *Supra* Note-69.
88. (1994) 3 SCC 569: 1994 SCC (Cri) 899.
89. AIR 1994 SC 1229.
90. AIR 1995 SC 1976.
91. *Supra* Note-86.
92. (1996) 4 SCC 33.
93. *Ibid.*
94. *Supra* Note-92.
95. (1996) 3 SCC 422.
96. AIR 1997 SC 3400.
97. AIR 1998 SC 3281.

98. *Ibid.*
99. (2000) 10 SCC 68.
100. (2001) 7 SCC 318 : 2001 SCC (Cri) 1009: AIR 2001 SC 3173.
101. (2001) 4 SCC 355.
102. (2002)4 SCC 247.
103. (2002) 2 SCC 210.
104. (08/09/2003), 2003(6) AD(Del) 486.
105. (08/09/2003), 2003(6) AD(Del) 591.
106. 2004(1) Crimes 171.

3

Factors Behind the Delay in Justice Delivery System in India

Factors behind the delay in the disposal of cases

1. Procedural Factors
   - 1.1 Pre-trial Delays
     - A. Delay in Investigation
     - B. Delay in Service of Summons
     - C. Delay in Filing of Written Submissions and Documents
     - D. Delay in Framing Issues/Charges
   - 1.2 Delay during Trial
     - A. Adjournment for Petty Reasons
     - B. Non-attendance of Witnesses
     - C. Lengthy Oral Arguments
     - D. Absence of lawyers
     - E. Application at Any Stage
     - F. Delayed Pronouncement of Judgment
   - 1.3 Delay during the Appellate Proceedings
   - 1.4 Delay during Execution Proceedings
2. Substantive Factors
   - 2.1 Judicial Vacancies

In a democratic country like India, for protecting and enhancing the rights of the people, the judiciary besides the legislature and the executive plays an important role. For the enforcement of rights of citizens and remedies thereto, in case of violation thereof, Courts have been established at all levels in the country. These courts by interpreting the laws enhance justice to the individual and the society at large. With the rapid growth in the population as well as technological and industrial advancement, the workload of the judiciary has increased tremendously. According to 2007 records, a total of around **2.9 crore** cases in various courts were pending. Out of this, **2,5285,982** cases were pending in the district and subordinate courts as on **31st December, 2007; 37,00,223** in the High Courts as on **31st December, 2007** and **46,926** in the Supreme Court as on **31st Dec. 2007.**[1] As per a latest report, there are 3.13,65,409 total number of cases pending in all the courts in India. The number of pending cases in the Supreme Court is 63,843 as on May 2014. It is 4.4 million in the high courts as on December 2013.

In a step towards creating a speedy justice delivery system, 2014 will see the Supreme Court of India working more than in 2013. In a bid to lessen the pendency of cases that has already crossed the mark of three crores, Chief Justice of India P. Sathasivam has cut down the number of holidays of the Supreme Court from 2014 onwards.[2]

With the increase in the workload, the efficiency of the courts is hampered badly. With the piling of pending cases and delay in the pronouncement of judgments, the saying 'Justice delayed is Justice denied' is truly applicable to our society. Due to this delay in rendering justice people are losing faith in the judicial system. The Supreme Court, from time to time, has confirmed that speedy trial is a fundamental right which is implied under **Article 21 of the Constitution**[3] but the position is still static and unchanged. Many committee and Boards set up by the Governments from time to time have suggested reformation and solutions for rendering justice effectively. However, the recommendations of these committees have not been put into practice due to one reason or the other.

The causes for delay in investigation and slip-shod investigation need to be taken stock of first in order to appreciate the problem in the proper perspective and to devise ways and means of checking the malady. Though the judiciary is not responsible for many delays that occur, in the public perception, it is the judiciary that is mainly responsible. Judiciary is mostly blamed without appreciating the real reasons. The judiciary, on its part, remains silent and refrains from conveying to the public that certain delays are beyond its control. This being the ground reality, what the judiciary is expected to do, is to introspect on the delays attributable to it and to vigorously undertake such measures, as are essential, to put its house in order. It is in this background that some essential remedial measures to be adopted by the judiciary are highlighted

FACTORS BEHIND DELAY IN THE DISPOSAL OF CASES

There is no one factor which is solely responsible for these arrears of cases. As is known that accumulation of tiny drops of water results into a pond, similarly a combination of plethora of factors contribute to the huge back-log of cases. There are a number of factors responsible for the delay; so for carrying out reforms in the existing scenario, a number of elements must be considered.

The impediments in the expeditious delivery of justice can be discussed under two broad headings: the procedural factors and the substantive factors.

1. PROCEDURAL FACTORS

The Supreme Court has held that the right to speedy trial flowing from Article 21 encompasses all the stages, namely the stages of investigation, inquiry, trial, appeal, revision and retrial.[4] As far as the procedural factors behind the delay in disposal of cases are concerned, such delays may broadly be discussed under four headings: (a) Pre-trial delays, (b) delay during trial, (c) delay during the appellate proceedings, and (d) delay during the execution proceedings.

1.1 Pre-trial Delays

Pre-trial delays may be due to the following factors :

(a) Delay in investigation;
(b) Delay in service of summons;
(c) Delay in filing written submissions and documents; and
(d) Delay in framing issues/charges.

A. *Delay in Investigation*

One principal object of criminal law is to protect the society from crime by punishing the offenders. However, justice and fair play requires that no one can be punished without a fair trial. A person might be under a thick cloud of suspicion of guilt, he might even be caught red-handed and yet he is not to be punished unless and until he is tried and adjudged guilty by a competent Court.[5] Investigation is the first step on the basis of which prosecution files a case against the accused in the court which tries the accused for alleged offence. It includes all proceedings under Criminal Procedure Code for the collection of evidence by a police officer or by any person (other than a Magistrate) who is authorized by a Magistrate in this behalf.[6] The Supreme Court has held the investigation of an offence as generally consisting of:

- Proceeding to the spot;
- Ascertainment of facts and circumstances of the case;
- Discovery and arrest of the suspected offender;
- Collection of evidence relating to the commission of offence which may consists of—
  - The examination of various persons (including the accused) and the recording of their statements into writing, if the officer thinks fit.
  - The search of places or seizure of things considered necessary for the investigation or to be produced at the trial; and
- Formation of opinion as to whether on the material collected, the accused can be put to trial before a magistrate and if so, taking necessary steps for the same by filing of a charge sheet under **section 173**.[7]

For the effective discharge of its duties, police has the power to arrest any person in certain circumstances. Arrest of an alleged offender even before summons or warrants are issued against him by the magistrate is provided so as to secure his presence during the trial. Police may take long time for investigation into an offence and thus delaying the initiation of the process of trial, which begins on the filing of charge sheet by the prosecution in court. In order to check this, Criminal Procedure Code imposes certain restrictions with respect to time to be taken by police for investigation by police and incarceration of the accused pending such investigation.[8]

Perusal of **Section 167(1)** of Criminal Procedure Code indicates that the investigation is expected to be completed within 24 hours of arrest of the accused. In case it appears that the investigation cannot be completed within 24 hours and the allegation against the accused is well founded, the investigation officer has to forward the diary entries along with the accused to the magistrate in order to seek further custody of the accused. At this stage, the magistrate can extend the period of detention of the accused by 15 days, which can further be extended to 60 or 90 days depending upon the gravity of offence. The accused becomes entitled to be released on bail on the expiry of the period of 60 or 90 days as the case may be.[9]

The police officers are required to complete investigation without unnecessary delay.[10] On the completion of investigation if there is not sufficient evidence or reasonable ground of suspicion, the accused is to be released on executing a bond to appear if and when so required before a magistrate empowered to take cognizance.[11] If there is sufficient evidence or reasonable ground of suspicion then the officer in charge of the police station forwards the accused under custody to a magistrate empowered to take cognizance of the offence upon a police report and to try the accused or commit him for trial. On completion of investigation, the officer in charge of the police station is also required to send a report to a competent magistrate. Such a report is known as 'police report'[12] popularly called "charge-sheet" or "Challan". When a charge sheet is filed in a case in respect of which there is sufficient evidence to forward the accused person to a magistrate, then along with the charge sheet all the documents or their extracts on which the prosecution proposes to rely (other than those already sent to the magistrate during investigation) and statement of witnesses whom the persecution proposes to examine have to be forwarded to the magistrate.

Despite the mandate of all these provisions requiring speedy investigation but hardly these are hardly followed and investigations go on for months after months without filing any chargesheet. Such delay in the filing of chargesheet results into delay in the commencement of trial which ultimately causes delay in the final disposal of cases.

B. Delay in Service of Summons

Fair trial requires that trial proceedings are conducted in the presence of the accused and that he is given a fair chance to defend himself. Further, in case the accused is found guilty at the conclusion of the trial, he must be available in person to receive the sentence passed on him. The presence of the accused at the trial can well be ensured by simply arresting and detaining him during the trial. However, this course should not be resorted to in every case on the broad principle that the liberty of a person should not be taken away without just cause. Moreover, the detention of the accused prior to the trial is likely to cause direct or indirect obstruction in the preparation of his defence. Consequently, the provisions regarding the issue of summons or of a warrant of arrest are aimed at ensuring the presence of the accused at his trial. But it is a common sight that the summons are not served in time. Delay in the delivery of summons also contributes to delay in the process of commencement of trial. A summon is an authoritative call to appear in court for a certain purpose. The summons from the court may be to the accused or to a witness to produce document or to a person to show cause.[13]

Every summon issued by a court under Criminal Procedure Code shall be issued in writing, in duplicate, signed by the presiding officer of such court or by such other officer as the High Court may from time to time by rule direct and shall bear the seal of the Court.[14] Every summon shall be served by a police officer or subject to such rules as the state Government may make in this behalf, by an officer of the Court issuing it or other public servant.[15] The summons shall, if practicable, be served personally on the person summoned, by delivering or tendering to him one of the duplicates of the summons.[16]

Sec. 91(1) provides that whenever any court or any officer in charge of a police station considers that the production of any document or other thing is necessary or desirable for the purpose of any investigation, inquiry or other proceedings under this code by or before such court or officer, such court may issue a summons or a written order to the person in whose possession or power such document or thing is believed to be, requiring him to attend and produce it, or to produce it, at the time and place stated in the summons or order.

14th Law Commission Report[17] pointed out that the Magistrate generally sends a packet containing summons by post to the concerned police station within whose jurisdiction the witness resides. Generally no record is kept by the station house officer to show the receipt of the packet of summons. Often the police officers allege that the summons were not received by them or did not reach them in time to effect service.

C. Delay in Filing of Written Submissions and Documents

Written submissions and documents submitted by parties in a case play a vital role in the decision of the case. But it is very common that the counsels for the parties do not submit these on time on one pretext or the other. In such a situation, judges are handicapped and they have no option but to postpone the hearing of the case.

D. Delay in Framing Issues/Charges

Delay in framing issues (in civil matters) and charges (in criminal matters) also pave the way for delay. Issue means a point in question; an important subject of debate, disagreement. Issues arise when a material proposition of fact or law is affirmed by one party and denied by the other. Material propositions are those propositions of law or fact which a plaintiff most allege in order to show a right to sue or a defendant must allege in order to constitute his defence.[18]

The machinery of a civil court is set in motion by the presentation of a plaint, which is the first stage of trial. The second stage is the filing of the written statement by the defendant. The third important stage in the suit is the framing and settlement of issues and the day on which such issues are framed is the first hearing of the suit.[19] But due to some reason or the other, the Court takes too much time in framing issues which ultimately results in delay in the final disposal of the suit.

Under the present stage of civilization, it has been universally accepted as a human value that a person accused of any offence should not be punished unless he has been given a fair trial and his guilt has been proved beyond reasonable doubt in such trial. The notion of fair trial, like all other concepts incorporating fairness or reasonableness, cannot be explained in absolute terms. Fairness is a relative concept and therefore, fairness in criminal trial could be measured only in relation to the gravity of the accusation, the time and resources which the society can reasonably afford to spend, the quality of available resources, the prevailing social values, etc.[20]

One basic requirement of a fair trial in criminal cases is to give precise information to the accused as to the accusation against him. This is vitally important to the accused in the preparation of his defense. Charges serve the purpose of notice or intimation to the accused, drawn up according to the specific language of law, giving clear and unambiguous or precise notice of the nature of accusation that the accused is called upon to meet in the course of trial.[21] So, unless charges are framed, the trial cannot begin and more often than not, the courts take too much time in framing charges either due to delay in submitting charge sheet by the investigating police officer or due to some other reason and the same result into delay in the commencement of the trial. For example, in the **Uphaar Fire Tragedy Case**, CBI filed chargesheets against the accused in 1997 but the Court framed charges in 2001.

1.2 Delay during Trial

Delay is also caused during the trial. Trial means the process undertaken for the judicial determination as to guilt or innocence of any person accused of any offence and such trial may be deemed to begin at the stage at which the court takes cognizance of an offence.

Delay during trial may be discussed under the following heads—

(i) Provisions for adjournment;
(ii) Non-attendance of witnesses;
(iii) Absence of lawyers;
(iv) Lengthy oral arguments;
(v) Application at any stage; and
(vi) Delayed pronouncement of judgments.

A. *Provision for Adjournment*

One of the main reasons that have resulted into pending cases is the adjournments granted by the court on flimsy grounds. **Sec. 309** of the **Code of Criminal Procedure**[22] and **Rule I, Order XVII** of the **Code of Civil Procedure** deals with adjournment and the power of the Court to postpone the hearing. Though, the Code of Criminal

Procedure does not talk of the maximum number of adjournments which can be granted but the Civil Procedure Code limits the same to three. Under the Code of Criminal Procedure the postponement or adjournment can be for such time as the court considers reasonable. What is reasonable time in a given case will depend upon the facts and circumstances of the case. The discretion to postpone or adjourn the case is to be exercised judicially and not arbitrarily.

Rule I, Order XVII of the **Code of Civil Procedure** provides that the court may, if sufficient cause is shown, at any stage of the suit, grant time to the parties or to any of them and may, from time to time adjourn the hearing of the suit for reasons to be recorded in writing, provided that no such adjournments shall be granted **more than three times** to a party during hearing of the suits. In every such case, the court shall fix a day for the further hearing of the suit and shall make such orders as to costs occasioned by the adjournment or such higher costs as the court deems fit.

Provided that—

(a) When the hearing of the suit has commenced, it shall be continued from day-to-day until all the witnesses in attendance have been examined, unless the court finds that for exceptional reasons to be recorded by it, adjournment of the hearing beyond the following day is necessary.

(b) No adjournment shall be granted at the request of a party, except where the circumstances are beyond the control of that party.

(c) The fact that pleader of a party is engaged in another court, shall not be a ground for adjournment.

(d) Where the illness of a pleader or his inability to conduct the case for any reason, other than his being engaged in another court, is put forward as a reason for seeking adjournment, the court shall not grant adjournment unless it is satisfied that the party applying for adjournment couldn't have engaged another pleader in time.

(e) Where a witness is present in court but a party or his pleader is not present or the party or his pleader, though present in court, is not ready to examine or cross-examine the witness, the court may, if it thinks fit, record the statement of the witness and pass such orders as it thinks fit.[23]

An adjournment may be granted by a court *inter alia* on the grounds of sickness of either party, his witnesses, or his counsel, non-service of summons, reasonable time for the preparation of the case, withdrawal of the counsels at the last moment, inability of a counsel to conduct the case, inability of a party to engage another counsel, etc. Again adjournment may be refused by the court *inter alia* on the grounds of engagement of a counsel in another court, dilatory conduct of the party, non-examination of a witness present in the court, abuse of process of the court, undertaking by the party on earlier occasion to proceed with the matter, inconvenience to the opposite party or his witnesses, the case being very old, the arguments of the other side is already concluded, etc. But to grant or refuse adjournment is at the discretion of the court. The power to grant or not to grant adjournment is not subject to any definite rules, but it should be exercised judicially and reasonably and after considering the facts and circumstances of each case.[24] So the adjournments are to be granted by the court only when the court deem necessary or advisable for reasons to be recorded. These provisions also give discretion to the court to grant adjournment subject to payment of costs. However, these conditions are not strictly followed and the bad practice continues not only by litigant but by sitting judges also. Such adjournment thwarts the right to speedy trial. By granting regular adjournments, the value of time and importance of the remedy sought for the cause of action get degraded. 'Justice is called justice' when it in the real sense delivers justice to the victim within a reasonable time.

B. Non-attendance of Witnesses

Non-attendance of witnesses also plays a part in the delay. The parties to the suit have to present in court a list of witnesses whom they propose to call either to give evidence or to produce documents and to obtain summonses for their attendance in the court. Such list must be filed on or before such date as the court may fix but not later than fifteen days after the issues are framed.[25] The object underlying this provision is going to give notice to the opposite party about the witnesses which his adversary is to examine in the case so that he could be in a position to know the nature of evidence he has to meet. Delay occurs firstly when the party or parties make unreasonable delay in presenting the list of witnesses and secondly, when the witnesses fail to comply with the summons and do not attend the court or refuse to depose.

The court has power to enforce the attendance of any person to whom a summons has been issued and for that purpose, may (a) issue a warrant for his arrest; (b) attach and sell his property; (c) impose a fine upon him not exceeding five thousand rupees; and order him to furnish security for his appearance and default commit him to the civil prison.[26]

C. *Lengthy Oral Argument*

Oral arguments, though a necessity for submissions before the Court, have been found to be unwieldy and time-consuming. Both Criminal Procedure Code and Civil Procedure Code discourage lengthy oral arguments. Any party to a proceeding may, as soon as may be, after the closure of his evidence, address concise oral arguments, and may, before he concludes the oral arguments, if any ,submit a memorandum of to the court setting forth concisely the arguments in support of his case.[27] The court may, if it is of the opinion that the oral arguments are not concise or relevant, regulate such arguments.[28] A court may permit a party or his pleader to argue a case orally. For such oral arguments, it is open to the court to fix time limit, as it thinks fit.[29]

Although both Criminal Procedure Code and Civil Procedure Code, empower the courts to regulate the length of oral arguments, but it is seen that the judges do not usually fix time limit for such oral arguments and the unnecessary oral arguments go on consuming precious time of the courts. So the judges should specify the time allocated to each side in advance. No case should be heard for full working hours in a day. It is required that written submissions including the case law to be relied upon, must be submitted to the Court. This will effectively reduce the length of oral arguments and considerably save the time of Court so as to make it available for attending to large number of pending cases.[30]

Further, since the Counsel charges daily fees for appearance in the Court the cost of litigation mounts in direct proportion to the length of the oral arguments. If one combines the fallout of oral arguments however, reverential approach one may have to the oral arguments, it is high time to curb and control the length of oral arguments.

D. *Absence of Lawyers/Pleader*

Absence of lawyers on the scheduled date of hearing also adds to the cases getting prolonged. The lawyer of a party may remain absent from the hearing of the case on one pretext or the other which are with -in the provisions of law like the death of his relative, or ill-health, but on the hindsight his absence may be due to non-preparation of the case or his engagement in another Court. In such a situation, the judge is constrained to adjourn the case. The Code of Civil Procedure and Code of Criminal Procedure are based on a general principle that, as far as possible, no proceeding in a court of law should be conducted to the detriment of any party in his absence. Civil Procedure Code requires the parties to attend the court in person or by their pleaders on the day fixed in the summons for the defendant to appear.[31] Where a plaintiff or a defendant, who has been ordered to appear in person, doesn't appear in person or show sufficient cause for non-appearance, the court may dismiss the suit, if he is the plaintiff, or proceed *ex parte*, if he is the defendant. Where the court has adjourned the hearing of the suit *ex parte*, and the defendant, at or before such hearing, appears and assigns good reasons for his previous non-appearance, the court may hear him upon such terms as it directs as to cost or otherwise.

E. *Application at any Stage*

There is a practice among the counsels to file applications at any stage of the proceedings of the case. They may do so in the guise of submitting some documents or making some amendments in the pleadings which, what they call, vital for the consideration of the court before disposal of the case. In this regard the existing laws also help them. For example, there is a provision in the Code of Civil Procedure which provides that the court may at any stage of the proceedings allow either party to alter or amend his pleadings in such manner and on such terms as may be just, and all such amendments shall be made as may be necessary for the purpose of determining the real questions in controversy between the parties.[32] By way of amendment, a rider has been imposed on the amendment of pleadings which provides that no application for amendment shall be allowed after the trial has commenced, unless the court comes to the conclusion that inspite of diligence, the party could not have raised the matter before the commencement of trial.[33] But the effect remains the same because all the counsels who want amendment in the pleadings take the plea that inspite of due diligence they failed to raise the matter before the commencement of the trial. But as a matter of fact, most of the time they do so for buying time foreseeing that they might loose the case. Such a practice causes substantial delay in the final disposal of cases because the filing of applications and new documents have to go through the dilatory process of filing, notice to the opposite party, arguments, order, appeal, etc.[34]

F. Delayed Pronouncement of Judgment

Justice should not only be done but should also appear to have been done. Similarly whereas justice delayed is justice denied, justice withheld is even worse than that. The inordinate, unexplained and negligent delay in pronouncing the judgment is alleged to have actually negatived the right of appeal conferred upon the convicts under Criminal Procedure Code. A right of appeal to meet the requirement of **Art. 21 of the Constitution** cannot be made a fraud by protracting the pronouncement of the judgment for reasons which are not attributable either to the litigant or to the State or to the legal profession.[35]

The intention of the legislature regarding the pronouncement of judgment can be inferred from the provisions of Criminal Procedure Code. **Section 353(1)** provides that the judgment in every trial in any criminal court of original jurisdiction, shall be pronounced in open court immediately after the conclusion of the trial or at a subsequent time for which due notice shall be given to the parties or their pleaders. The words "some subsequent time" mentioned in this section is very important because it contemplates the passing of the judgment without delay, as delay in the pronouncement of the judgment is opposed to the principles of law.[36]

It is true that for High Courts, no period for the pronouncement of judgment is provided either under the Civil Procedure Code and Criminal Procedure Code but as pronouncement of judgment is a part of the justice dispensing system, it has to be without delay. In a country like ours where people consider the Judges only second to God, efforts should be made to strengthen that belief of the common people. Delay in disposal of cases cause the people to raise eyebrows. It is seen that some judges don't deliver judgments even after a lapse of several months after hearing. This may be to buy time for preparing the judgment. This not only causes delay but also shakes the confidence of the people in the judicial system.[37]

1.3 Delay during the Appellate Proceeding

Human judgment is not infallible. Despite all the provisions for ensuring a fair trial and a just decision, mistakes are possible and errors cannot be ruled out. The Code therefore, provides for "appeals" and "revision" and thereby enables the superior Courts to review and correct the decisions of the lower Courts. Apart from it being a corrective device, review procedure serves another important purpose. The very fact that the decision of the lower Courts is duly scrutinized by a superior court in "appeal" or "revision" gives satisfaction to the party aggrieved by that decision. It assures the aggrieved party that all reasonable efforts have been made to reach a just decision free from plausible errors, prejudices and mistakes.

Although this review procedure through "appeal or revision" is imperative for correctional justice but too much recourse to such procedure is causing another problem, that is, **delay in final disposal of cases**. The reason is that the superior Courts are busy in deciding appeals leaving the regular matters at bay. Further, the Superior Courts take too much time in deciding appeals which is partly due their workload and mostly due to delay in getting the files from the trial court whose decision is challenged. If the multiplicity of appeals are to be reduced and higher courts are to function burden less and discharge effective judicial functioning in the direction of progressive evolution of law, judicial officers at the district level have to discharge their functions diligently so as to avoid shortcomings in their decisions.

1.4 Delay during Execution Proceedings

The duty of a Court is not over by the mere pronouncement of a decree or order. The Court has to see that fruits of the decree or order reach to the person in favour of whom the decision has been given. But pronouncements of the Courts are not backed by administrative authority/machinery of the State for effective execution. This keeps the Courts busy in ordering the administrative authorities to carry out the execution of the Court's order. Delay is also caused when a decree is sent for execution to another court because such a court is required to supply to the executing court a copy of the decree along with some other certificates.[38] But such documents are not provided in time to such executing Courts which thereby cause delay in the execution of the decree. Further there is a provision for stay of execution of the decision so as to enable the person against whom the decision has been given to appeal against the decision.[39] These things results delay in the final disposal of the cases, thereby adding to the huge backlog of cases.

2. SUBSTANTIVE FACTORS

It is not that the procedural factors are alone responsible for delay in disposal of cases; there are a number of substantive factors which contribute to the piling up of pending cases. These substantive factors may be discussed under the following heads:

2.1 Judicial vacancies/Delay in appointment of judges.
2.2 Lack of accountability of judges
2.3 Too many vacations in court
2.4 Misuse of PIL
2.5 Witnesses Turning hostile
2.6 Writ jurisdiction
2.7 Delay by the Judges.

2.1 Judicial Vacancies/Delay in Appointment of Judges

For clearing pending cases an adequate number of judges must be appointed and once the posts of judicial officers fall vacant, there shouldn't be unreasonable delay in the appointment rather they should be filled on a priority basis. But in the Indian judicial system, there are a number of vacancies existing which ultimately affects the efficiency of rendering justice. The former chief Justice of India S.P. Bharocha on this account had said that "It is only when we have far more trial courts functioning that we shall be able to dispose of more cases than are being filed and thus cut down on arrears." In 2002, the total strength of judges in the High Courts was 669 out of which there were 163 vacancies which come out to be 25% of the total strength. It was also suggested by the 127th Law Commission Report, 1988[40] that the judge population ratio should be increased from 10 judges per million populations (at that time) to 50 judges per million populations within a period of five years. The Supreme Court in *All India Judges' Association Case*[41] has directed the State and Central Governments to increase the strength of judges five times over a period of next five years. Due to this low judge-population ratio, the courts lack the requisite strength of judges to decide the pending cases. But the Government has neither taken any interest nor any steps to implement the said recommendation. The view of the Government is that raising the strength of the judges must be set on the basis of pendency of cases and the average rate of disposal of cases and not simply on the basis of population.

But filling the vacancy of judges is not the sole responsibility of the Government. The judiciary also plays a crucial role in the appointment of judges. The Supreme Court while interpreting **Articles 124 and 217** of the Constitution of India in its judgment in *Advocates on Record Association* v. *Union of India and others* [42] has held that a proposal for the appointment of a judge in the Supreme Court must be initiated by the Chief Justice of India and in the case of a High Court by its Chief Justice of a High Court to another High Court, the proposal has to be initiated by the Chief Justice of India.

Therefore, the judiciary is also responsible for not performing its duty of proposing the name for appointing judges to the government, which in turn would be sent to the President of India for approval. Also, according to norms, the process of filling up of vacancy should start 6 months before the actual date of retirement of a Judge, but this is hardly followed.

The present state of affairs regarding judicial vacancies has been aptly described by the President of Confederation of the Indian Bar **Mr. Praveen H. Parekh**. He said: "The Indian Judiciary consists of one Supreme Court with 26 judges, twenty-one (21) High Courts with a sanctioned strength of 725 judges but the working strength as on 1st March 2007 is 597 and 14,477 subordination Courts/Judges but the working strength is only 11,767 as on 1 March 2007".[43] As per a recent report published by Ministry of Law and Justice in year 2014 shows 24 high courts with a sanctioned strength of 950 but the working strength is 631. Supreme Court consists of 28 judges but the sanctioned is 31.

An immediate question one might ask from the above statistics is why such large number of vacancies are allowed to remain particularly at the trial court level where the arrear of cases is constantly mounting. That takes us to the selection and appointment process where the Government has a greater role to play than the judiciary. A way has to be found by the Government and the judiciary to address this problem in order to maintain a zero vacancy situation all the time. The Supreme Court through the Chief Justices

Annual conference has taken steps to implement such zero vacancy in the High Courts in this regard. This will certainly help to substantially increase the available judicial hours to attend pending work and reduce delays in the process.[44]

What are the minimum numbers of courts / judges required to deliver timely justice and to avoid pendency of cases for long periods. The judiciary has been conducting scientific studies through expert committees and otherwise to reach an objective and acceptable figure in this regard. One standard recommendation was to fix the maximum capacity a judge can possibly take in a given year and decide the requirement of judge strength based on average filing and accumulated years.

2.2 Lack of Accountability of Judges

The Constitution of India talks about free and independent judiciary which not only implies that the judicial organ of the state has been kept away from the intervention of the executive and legislature. The existence of a fearless and independent judiciary is founded in the constitutional structure of India. A notable feature of the Indian Constitution is that it accords a dignified and crucial position to the judiciary in India. In the celebrated decision of the Supreme Court in *S.P. Gupta* v. *Union of India*,[45] it was held that; "The concept of independent of the judiciary is a noble concept which inspires the constitutional scheme and constitutes the foundation on which rests the edifice of our democratic polity. If there is one principle which runs through the entire fabric of the constitution, it is the principle of the rule of law under the constitution and it is the judiciary which is entrusted with the task of keeping every organ of the state within the limits of the law thereby making the rule of law meaningful and effective."[46] This, however, at no stage means that judiciary is not accountable to the nation. In a democracy, the power lies with the people. The Supreme Court in a number of cases[47] held that Courts are accountable to the people of the country and so the judiciary must concern itself with this fact while functioning. Contrary to what has been envisaged in the constitution, judges play at their own whims as far as their duties in the courts are concerned and thereby adds to the delay in the disposal of cases. Under **Art. 235** [48] of the constitution of India, High Courts have the power of control over Subordinate Courts but the Supreme Court has no such power over High Courts. The Chief Justice of

India/High Courts has no power to control or make accountable other judges of the court.

Judicial behaviour has been receiving attention especially since 1998 when a former judge of the Supreme Court observed that: "everything was rotten about the Indian judiciary." To a query, why the judge did not say this while he was in office, the reply was: "I was afraid of the safety of my life and children." These statements conceal more than what they reveal. If the power-holder in the judiciary has had to feel so badly and so strongly, there obviously is some rot somewhere.[49]

The concept of judicial accountability has three stages. First, each member of the judiciary has the accountability to himself. He has to do a soul searching and self-introspection. He has to convince himself that what he has done is morally and more importantly legally correct and his decision is not dictated by any extraneous consideration. As Lord Donaldson, the former English Master of Rolls said; "Judges are without constituency and answerable to no one except to their conscience and the law. The second stage of accountability is the accountability of the individual to the institution. Here again, self-introspection and soul searching plays a vital role. The individual judge has to ensure that what he has done would not bring disrespect or disrepute to the institutions. On the contrary, even if it may not increase the respectability and credibility of the institution, it shall not diminish it. The institution cannot be segregated from the individuals. The credibility or lack of credibility would depend to a compete measure on the individuals. The third stage is the most important one. It is the accountability of the institution to the society. Judges have their accountability to the society and their accountability must be judged from the conscience and oath to their office, i.e., they have to defend and uphold the constitution and the laws without fear and favour. Any criticism about the judicial system or judges, which hampers the administration of justice or erodes the faith on the system and brings it to ridicule must be prevented. Every citizen has a responsibility to ensure that the line between measured criticism of judgments and denigration of judges is not traversed. Constitutionalism is not enhanced by hostility directed against the judiciary, which plays a pivotal role in maintaining the rule of law. [50]

Our Indian system of accountability is based on the basic premise that human beings are not infallible and judges are not exception to that, and if the error is not ill-motivated then the same can be corrected by the exercise of appellate or review powers and warrants no personal accountability of the judges. However, the judges are accountable for their conduct in public or private life if such conduct amounts to 'misbehaviour' or brings disrepute or dishonour to the judiciary. Mr. Somnath Chatterjee, the Former Speaker of Lok Sabha, once said, " We hold the judiciary in high esteem ... Judges are assumed to be men of honesty and integrity and discharge their duties and functions with a sense of fairness and independence without fear or favour." So judges are expected to show highest form of standards in their conduct. In India it is an undoubted fact that corruption has infected the judiciary also. Corruption brings disrepute to the institution of judiciary, reduces public confidence in courts, leads also to unpredictability of judicial decision and thereby undermines the effectiveness of the institution.[51]

The Right to Information Act, 2005 was passed in India with the objective of promoting transparency in governance. The Act provides that every public authority shall provide access to its documents and proceedings.[52] The Act defines 'public authority' as any and everybody constituted under the constitution or any other law of the government.[53] But, unfortunately judiciary is seeking to effectively remove itself from the purview of the Right to Information Act, 2005. The Right to Information Act, if implemented in the judicial domain, it will provide right to information for judicial as well as administrative functions of the court and will enhance judicial accountability in the system.[54]

The **Woolf Report** emphasized to make the judiciary accountable for their functioning by generating accurate judicial statistics revised on daily basis. It was observed by the committee that statistic report pertaining to the functioning of judges and flow of such information ultimately make judges more accountable to the judiciary. It was also suggested that it is more important and useful to tackle the arrears rather than increasing financial and human resources. But these suggestions remain on paper and have never been put into practice.[55]

The Annual Report of Ministry of Law, Justice and Company Affairs has given data about judicial arrears and nothing about the nature of cases pending. So, it is not fruitful to deal with the pendency of cases. There must be some judicial database that includes the details about the specific laws which deals with subject matter, sections, legal nature of dispute, time taken to decide the case, interim relief in operation and number of adjournments granted, etc.[56]

2.3 Too Many Vacations in Courts

The most debated question relating to the causes of delay is the Court vacations. In India, long vacations in Courts are a unique feature. If courts in other countries can function like any other business establishment, then why cannot, courts in India do so?

The table below makes a comparison between the working days and time of different courts and Government and private establishment:[57]

Sl. No.	*Supreme Court*	*High Court*	*District Subordinate courts*	*Other Government Establishment*	*Private Org./Non-Government*
1.	185 days a year	210 days a year	240 days a year	245 days a year	255 days a year
2.	10.30 am to 4.00 pm with one hour lunch i.e. Four hours 30 minutes each working day	10.30 am to 4.30 pm with one hour lunch i.e. Five hours each working day	10.30 am to 5.00 pm with 45 minutes lunch i.e. Five hours 45 minutes each working day	10.00 am to 5.45 pm with 45 minutes lunch i.e. Seven hours a day	9.30 am to 6.00 pm with 30 minutes lunch i.e. 8 hours or more each working day

The system of vacations is a legacy of the colonial rule. In the pre-independence period, the burden was not so great in comparison to the present situation. Also, the English coming from cold climate found the summer in India unbearable. Therefore, vacations were a kind of an arrangement to enable them to go to England during summer and spend the time comfortably. That was the time when traveling was done by sea which required several weeks. This appears to be the real reason for the introduction of long vacations for courts in India.[58] Now the situation has been changed drastically and the courts are over burdened with pending cases. So, the situation demands that the courts should do away with such long vacations and work as other Government establishments do.[59]

In a step towards creating a speedy justice delivery system, 2014 will see the Supreme Court of India working more than in 2013. In a bid to lessen the pendency of cases that has already crossed the mark of three crores, Chief Justice of India P Sathasivam has cut down the number of holidays of the Supreme Court from 2014 onwards.[60]

2.4 Misuse of PIL

The traditional rule is that right to move the courts is only available to those whose fundamental rights are infringed. The power vested in the Supreme Court can only be exercised for the enforcement of fundamental rights. But this traditional rule of *locus standi* that a petition under **Art. 32** can only be filed by a person whose fundamental right is infringed has now been considerably relaxed by the Supreme Court. The Court now permits public spirited citizens for the enforcement of constitutional or other legal rights of any person or group of persons who because of their poverty or socially or economically disadvantaged position are unable to approach the court for relief.

In *A.B.S.K. Sangh (Rly)* v. *Union of India*[61], the Supreme Court held that the Akhil Bhartiya Sarkari Karmachari Sangh (Railway) though an unregistered association could maintain a writ petition under Art 32 for the redressal of a common grievance. Thus, Art. 32 is not confined to protect only individual's fundamental rights but is capable of doing justice wherever the society has an interest in it. Krishna Iyer J. observed:

> "*Access to justice through 'Class actions', 'public interest litigation' and 'representative proceeding' is the present constitutional jurisprudence*".

In the *Judges Transfer case*[62] a seven-judge Bench of the S.C. has set at rest the controversy as to whether a person who is not directly involved in a case can move the court for enforcement of constitutional or other legal rights of any person or group of persons who because of their poverty or socially or economically disadvantaged position are unable to approach the court for relief. The court held that any member of the public having 'sufficient interest' can approach the court for enforcing constitutional or legal right of other persons and for redressal of a common grievance.

Bhagwati J. observed:

> "We would, therefore, held that any member of the public having sufficient interest can maintain an action for judicial redress for public injury arising from breach of public duty or

from violation of some provision of the constitution or law and seek enforcement of such public duty and observance of such constitutional or legal provisions. This is absolutely necessary for maintaining rule of law, furthering the cause of justice and accelerating the pace of realization of the constitutional objectives".

Although PIL has been a revolutionary step in rendering justice to the poor but of late the same is filed for getting publicity, thereby increasing the workload of courts. This ultimately cause delay in disposal of regular cases. While expanding the scope of the 'locus standi' rules, his lordship Bhagwati J. (as he then was) expressed a note of caution. He observed:

"But we must be careful to see that the members of the public, who approach the courts in cases of this kind, is acting bonafide and not for personal gain or private profit or political motivation or other oblique considerations. The court must not allow its process to be abused by politicians and others......."

In *Sachidanand Pandey* v. *State of West Bengal*,[63] Justice Khalid observed:

"If the court do not restrict the free flow of such cases in the name of public interest litigation, the traditional litigation will suffer and the courts of law, instead of dispensing justice, will have to take upon themselves administrative and executive functions".

In *Janta Dal* v. *H.S. Chaudhary*[64] Justice Pandian made the following observation:

"........*only a person acting bonafide and having interest in the proceeding of PIL will alone have a locus standi and can approach the court to wipeout the tears of the poor and needy, suffering from violation of their fundamental rights, but not a person for personal gain or private profit. Similarly, a* vexatious petition under the colour of PIL brought before the court for vindicating any personal grievance, deserve rejection at the threshold".

In spite of its beneficial effect, the PIL is subject to criticism mainly on the ground that the Courts are flooded with litigations resulting in delay in deciding many other important cases and this criticism is not far from truth because the courts are finding it difficult to handle the arrears of cases.

2.5 Hostile Witnesses

The problem of witnesses turning hostile in important cases have become a major problem in rendering due justice by our criminal justice system. Bentham said "witnesses are the eyes and ears of justice. Their statements have a magic force to change the entire case". Of the many things that plague the criminal justice system in India, and thereby increasing the backlog of cases in our country, the most overwhelming and important one is the fact that our conviction rate is very low which is at about 6%. The basic reason for such poor conviction rate is that it is difficult "to prove beyond reasonable doubt" the fact that it was the accused and only the accused who committed the offence. So it requires witnesses to prove the guilt of the accused. In common parlance, witness is understood as 'a person who has some knowledge about the dispute' and his duty is to appear in the court and testify truthfully. In *Charan Singh* v. *State of Punjab*, Wadhwa J. observed:

> "a criminal case is built on the edifice of evidence, that is admissible in law, for that witnesses are required whether direct or indirect or circumstantial evidence. *By giving evidence, he performs sacred duty of assisting the court to discover the truth*".
>
> (Emphasis supplied)

The procedural law envisages that administration of oath to the witness precedes the recording of the testimony of the witness. He is not supposed to withdraw from the given statement and the witness ought to sustain the legal sanctity and ethos of the evidence. But with the decline of moral values, the sanctity of Oath is completely bruised and so a witness resiling from the statement has become a common feature of the criminal trial. People are accustomed to utter falsehood in Courts. Intimidation, subornation, vengeance, or some expectation of benefits etc. may be the traditional causes of deviation in witness testimony. Pain of repeated and numerous court visits may also frustrate the witness to resort to casual attitude to the truth. In cases of faction feuds, rivalry between potential and powerful people, where there may be fear of life and safety, witnesses lose their moral conviction before the dreadful scenario of factual conditions.

Whatever may be the reason, the courts cannot remain complacent and passive listeners and recorders of witness version.[65]

The number of witnesses turning hostile is increasing in cases concerning grave offences. Some such incidents are the famous **BMW case, Jessica Lal murder case and Best Bakery case**. The first one was regarding the BMW car running over six people in the early morning hours. The accused in this case was 22 years old, Sanjeev Nanda, grandson of former Naval Chief S.M. Nanda. The two key prosecution witnesses subsequently changed their version and said that they saw a truck, and not a BMW hitting the victims.

The second case involved the murder of a model, **Jessica Lal** who was shot at point blank range amidst a big party thrown at a Delhi restaurant. Here the accused was Manu Sharma who hails from an affluent family and had political connections. In this case, all the three witnesses have turned hostile one by one, thereby delaying the final disposal of the case. Although finally Manu Sharma has been convicted but due to witnesses turning hostile, final disposal of the case took a long time.

In the landmark verdict in *Best Bakery Case*[66] the Supreme Court gave an enlightened observation and sent the key witness Zahira Sheikh to the jail for playing fraud on the court by turning hostile. Holding her in contempt, the Supreme Court Bench observed that:

> "In a criminal case, the fate of the proceedings cannot always be left entirely in the hands of the parties, crime being public wrong in breach and violation of public rights and duties, which affect the whole community and are harmful to the society in general. The concept of fair trial entails familiar triangulation of interests of the accused, the victim and the society and therefore, it is the community that acts through the State and the prosecuting agencies. Interest of the society is not to be treated completely with disdain and as *persona non-grata*. Courts have always been considered to have an overriding duty to maintain public confidence in the administration of justice. Due administration of justice has always been viewed as a continuous process, not confined to determination of the particular case protecting its ability to function as a court of law in the future as in the case before it. If a criminal court is to be an effective instrument in dispensing justice, the presiding judge

must cease to be a mere spectator and a mere recording machine by becoming a participant in the trial evincing intelligent, active interest and elicit all relevant material necessary for reaching the correct conclusion and administer justice with fairness and impartially to the both parties of a particular case as well as to the society at large. Courts administering criminal justice cannot turn a blind eye to vexatious or oppressive conduct that has occurred in relation to proceedings, even if a fair trial is still possible, except at the risk of undermining the fair name and standing of the judges as impartial and independent adjudicators."

In most of the cases witnesses are purchased with the use of money. Generally those people who are extremely rich, industrialists, bureaucrats or high profile public servants or politicians who have committed the crime either accidentally or intentionally use this method. They are of the belief that their purchasing power is very high and thus they can afford to relax once the witness has been bought over. These types of cases occur all over India, but are mostly prevalent in the Metropolitan cities of the country.[67]

Very often muscle power is also used. Where money fails, muscles work. Even an honest law-abiding citizen would think hundred times before deposing against the accused if he or any of his family members is threatened with dire consequences or death. They have no option but to do so because most of them are habitual and crime is there profession. contract killers and men belonging to the underworld.[68]

Apart from money and muscle power there are various other ways in which witnesses are forced to turn hostile viz, political pressure, long winding Court procedures, the psychological factor, self-generating fear, etc. Whatever be the tactics applied by powerful ones in turning the witnesses hostile that undoubtedly makes way for delay in the expeditious delivery of justice.

2.6 Writ Petitions

With the increase in the socio-economic and welfare activities of the State and growing awareness of the citizen as to his rights, **Articles 32 and 226 of the Constitution** assumed singular importance in our system of administration of justice. It empowers the Supreme Court and High Courts throughout the territories, in relation to which it exercises jurisdiction, to issue to any person or authority directions or orders or writs including writs in the nature of *habeas corpus*, *mandamus*, prohibition, *quo warranto*, and *certiorari*, whichever is appropriate.[69]

Writ Petitions are extra-ordinary constitutional remedies under the Constitution by which the Judiciary reviews the executive and legislative acts. They don't constitute the normal judicial work of adjudicating disputes amongst citizens or between citizens and governments, etc .The situation has become increasingly serious even for the extra-ordinary remedies of writ petitions. Priorities have to be set even amongst the extra-ordinary remedies. Further, only the temporary, urgent, ad interim, or interim relief is ordered in writ petitions and the real and main issues are relegated to the background and may not be addressed for want of time. More often than not the writ petitions are filed to force the executive to do their duty and the Courts have to waste their precious time in giving direction to the executive to perform their constitutional duty due to which the disposal rate of cases is reduced substantially. Very often, a number of writ petitions are filed involving not only the same point of law but also the same or similar facts. The grouping of these petitions by the Registry will help in the quick and satisfactory disposal of cases. The co-operation of the various government departments would be required for the expeditious disposal of writ cases.

2.7 Delay by the Judges

Some practices of our judiciary also cause delay and arrears. Writing of lengthy judgments obscuring the ratio is not uncommon in India. A lot of time is consumed not only by the judges but by others also in writing the judgment which ultimately results in delay in pronouncement of the judgment. Writing separate judgments even when they are concurring makes the exercise time-consuming and confusing. It thereby becomes difficult to find the ratio in quick time.[70]

When judges give separate but concurring judgments they say that they want to give reasons other than those mentioned in the judgment with which they concur. However, more often than not it is seen that the most of the separate judgment do add that all have been discussed in the main judgment. The separate judgments may differ only in minor details, still it is written and published. It is not known what benefit one gets from the practice. The dissenting judgments on the contrary display clarity; it helps the lawyers and law students a lot in understanding the ratio as well as the unarticulated premises of the conclusion. The dissenting judgments of some of our well-known judges are really path-finders.[71]

The languages employed by the judges in writting judgments have also come for criticism. At times the judges who have a flair for flowery languages indulge in displaying good command over the language and in the process make others to miss the legal point discussed in the case. Such writings cause delay not only at the hands of the judges but also for lawyers in finding out the ratio of the decisions.

EMPIRICAL STUDY OF DELAY IN THE DISPOSAL OF CASES

The main objective of the empirical study is to ascertain the impediments behind the speedy trial. In other words, through this empirical study the researchers endeavours to find out the main reasons for delay in the disposal of cases.

. The study is confined to Courts of Delhi only, so the viewpoint of some of the litigants, lawyers and judicial officers of Patiala House Court, Tis Hazari Court, Delhi High Court and Supreme Court of India, have been taken on the basis of empirical investigation which have been carried out through schedule and interview method.

Findings of the Empirical Study

For a better understanding of the empirical study, the opinion of litigants, lawyers and Judicial officers can be discussed under several heads like nature of the pending case, year of filing the case, main reasons for the delay, personal experience of delay, designation of Judicial officers interviewed and other correlated issues.

The finding given below (in the tabulation A, B & C) is based on the data collected by the researcher from the litigants, lawyer and judicial officers.

ANALYSIS OF DATA

Analysis of Table A

As part of this empirical study, the researcher has interviewed ten litigants across the Courts in Delhi. On the question as to what

TABLE A
Response of Litigants

Sl. No.	*Nature of the Pending Cases*	*Whom the case was filled*	*Stage of the Case*	*Main Reason for the delay*	*How Many times*
1.	Civil	2001	Trial	Adjournment	Thrice
2.	Civil	1998	Appellate	Adjournment	Not known
3.	Civil	1991	Appellate	Adjournment	Thrice
4.	Civil	1994	Appellate	Adjournment	Not known
5.	Civil	1992	Appellate	Absence of the lawyer and Adjournment	Four times
6.	Criminal	2001	Trial	Adjournment	Six times
7.	Criminal	1995	Appellate	Adjournment	Eight times
8.	Motor accident claim case	2003	Trial	Adjournment	Thrice
9.	Criminal	2000	Appellate	Adjournment	Not exactly Known
10.	Criminal	2003	Trial	Adjournment	Thrice

TABLE B
Responses of Lawyers

Sl. No.	*Nature of cases dealt in by you*	*Year of start of profession*	*Personal experience of delay*	*Main reason for delay in disposal of cases*
1.	Both Civil and Criminal	1981	A civil case (property dispute) took 13 years for final disposal	Judges-population ratio low
2.	Criminal	1986	Rape case took 12 years for final disposal	Judicial vacancies in the subordinates courts
3.	Criminal	1981	Attempt to murder pending for 10 years	Awareness of rights by the common people

4.	Both Civil and Criminal	1978	Kidnapping case took 11 years	Judges-population ratio low
5.	Criminal pending for 10 year	1994	A case of murder Awareness of rights by common people	
6.	Civil	1979	Murder case took 15 year	Lack of Judicial officer in the lower court
7.	Both Civil and Criminal	1985	Criminal assault case took 7 years	Judicial Vacancies
8.	Both civil and criminal	1995	Murder case pending for 9 years	Heavy burden of cases much resources on courts
9.	Criminal	1999	A rape case pending for 7 years	Judicial vacancies
10.	Civil	2001	An illegal encroachment case pending for 7 years	Judicial population ratio low

Table C
Responses of Judicial Officers

Sl. No.	*Designation of the Judicial Officer*	*Year of appointment*	*Main reason for delay in the disposal of cases*
1.	ACMM (Additional Chief Metropolitan Magistrate)	1981	Lack of Judicial officer to handle the inflow of cases
2.	Presiding officer MCD Court	1980	Adjournment and frequent application for adding documents
3.	Judicial Magistrate 1st class	2001	Judges-Population ratio less
4.	Judicial Magistrate 1st class	2002	Lack of Judicial officers
5.	Presiding officers MACT	1989	Judges-population ratio less

is the main reason for delay; the respondents are more or less unanimous in their response. Out of these ten respondents, eight are of the view that the frequent adjournments on one ground or the other is the main reason for delay. Remaining two are of the view that absence of lawyers as well as adjournments are responsible for delay. But the bottom line is that the repeated adjournments are granted due to the fact that the courts are over-burdened with cases. Therefore the judicial officer does not object too much in granting adjournments because they have to take up other pending cases also on a priority basis.

Analysis of Table B

To know the views of lawyers as to the cause for delay in the disposal of cases, the researchers interviewed ten lawyers across the courts in Delhi. All these respondents are unanimous that there is on one factor responsible for delay but combination of several factors contribute to the delay. But on the question as to what is the main reason for delay, the respondents are more or less unanimous in their responses. Out of these ten respondents, three are of the view that the judges-population ratio is very low and this is the main factor for delay in the disposal of cases. India is amongst the lowest in the Judges Population ratio. The judge-population ratio in India is 10.5 Judges for every 10 lakh citizens. In contrast, there are 107 judges in the United States of America for every 10 lakh citizens. Another three respondents are of the view that the judicial vacancies is one the main reason for delay in the disposal of cases. Statistics reveal that the High Courts have a sanctioned strength of 749 Judges but the working strength is only 597 as on 1st March 2007. And the sanctioned strength of judicial officers in the subordinate courts is 14,477 but the working strength is only 11,767 as on 1st March 2007. That is to say that 152 posts of judges are lying vacant in the High Courts and around 3000 posts of judicial officers of subordinate courts are lying vacant without any effort on the part of the government to fill the same.

Out of the rest four respondents, three are of the view that awareness of rights by the common people have resulted in more litigation and thereby increasing the burden on courts but there is no corresponding increase in the number of Judicial officers to handle these cases. One respondent is of the opinion that lack of judicial officers is the main reason for delay because as a human being, they cannot handle more than a particular number of cases per day. So, all the respondents are more or less unanimous in their opinion that there should be an increase in the number of judicial officers to tackle the huge back log of cases.

Analysis of Table C

To know the opinion of judicial officers as to the cause for delay in the disposal of cases, the researchers interviewed five judicial officers of various courts in Delhi. Out of these five Judicial officers, two are of the opinion that low judge-population ratio is the main reason for delay. Out of the rest three, two are of the opinion that lack of judicial officers in comparison to inflow of cases is the main reason for huge backlog of cases. One such judge is of the opinion that filing of the cases are increasing geometrically while the number of Judicial officers are the same as it was five or ten years back. He is of the opinion that in order to dispose of pending cases in the present state of affair, a judicial officer have to dispose of one thousand cases per month, whereas it is humanely impossible for a Judicial officer to handle more than two hundred cases per month. One respondent is of the opinion that frequent adjournment of cases either due to false pretence by the lawyers or due to over burdening of courts also adds to the delay. He is of the opinion that some lawyers also resort to filing application for adding document with the intention of delaying the cases. One such judicial officers is of the opinion that in order to reduce the pendency of cases, there has to be a four-fold increase in the number of judicial officers.

3. CONCLUSION

After discussion and cogitation over various reasons for delay in the disposal of cases as well as after analyzing the pros and cons of the data, it can be said that there is no one single factor which is solely responsible for delay in disposal of cases rather it is the combination of several factors which are contributing to delay. But what is visible is that the lack of judicial officers and Judges is the main reason for delay in the disposal of cases. There is considerable increase in litigation, almost an explosion in numbers of litigations without any proportionate increase either in the number of Judge or Judicial Infrastructure. Another reason for delay (as pointed by the respondents) is the frequent adjournment of cases. But such adjournments are the direct fall out of the increasing inflow of cases. Sufficient judicial officers commensurate with the cases filed everyday are not there. Therefore, the judicial officers are constrained to adjourn the cases again and again so as to take up other matters also. In whatever way one approaches the problem , there is unanimity of opinion that the strength of judges in India has to be considerably increased to cope with the growing litigation and demands. So the need of the hour is to overhaul the entire system of justice delivery mechanism so that the problem of delay can be nipped in the bud.

Notes and References

1. Figure was given by Chief Justice K.G. Balakrishnan while inaugurating the "All India Seminar on Judicial Reform" held from 23rd - 25th Feb. 2008.
2. Coutsey http://www.newindianexpress.com/thesundaystandard/Supreme-Sacrifice-for-Speedy-Justice/2013/12/29/article1970479.
3. Art. 21 provides that "No person shall be deprived of his life and personal liberty except according to procedure established by law".
4. *A. R. Antulay v. R.S. Nayak*, (1992) 1 SCC 225.
5. R.V. Kelkar; *Criminal Procrdure Code;* 4th edition, 2004; p. 30.
6. Section 2(h).The Code of Criminal Procedure.
7. *H.N. Rishbud* v. *State of Delhi,* AIR 1955 SC 196.
8. *Abinandan Jha* v. *Dinesh Mishra*, AIR 1968 SC 117,120; 1968 Cri LJ 97.
9. S. 167(2), Proviso, Criminal Procedure Code.
10. S.173(1), Criminal Procedure Code, 1973.
11. S.169, Criminal Procedure Code, 1973.
12. S.2(r), Criminal Procedure Code, 1973.
13. Supra note-4, at p. 41.
14. S. 61, Criminal Procedure Code, 1973.
15. S. 62(1), Criminal Procedure Code, 1973.
16. S. 62(2) Criminal Procedure Code, 1973.
17. Law Commission of India, 14th Report, Vol. II; p. 780.
18. Order XIV, Rule 1-3, The Code of Civil Procedure.
19. *Sangram Singh* v. *Election Tribunal*, AIR 1955 SC 425.
20. Supra Note-4, at p. 320.
21. *V.C. Shukla* v. *State through CBI*, 1980 Supp SCC 92: 1980 SCC (Cri) 695.
22. **Sec 309(1) of Cr. P.C.** provides that in every inquiry or trial the proceedings shall be held as expeditiously as possible and in particular, when the examination of witnesses has once begun, the same shall be continued from day-to-day until at witnesses in attendance have been examined, unless the court finds the adjournment of the same beyond the following day to be necessary for reasons to be recorded.

    Sec. 309 (2) of Cr.P.C. provides that if the court after taking cognizance of an offence or commencement of trial, finds it necessary or advisable to postpone the commencement of or adjourn, any inquiry or trial, it may form time to time, for reasons to be recorded, postpone or adjourn the same on such terms as it thinks fit for such time as it consider reasonable and may by warrant remand the accused if in custody.

Provided that when witnesses are in attendance, no adjournment or postponement shall be granted, without examining them, except for special reasons to be recorded in writing.

Provided also that no adjournments shall be granted for the purpose only of enabling the accused person to show cause against the sentence proposed to be imposed on him.

23. Ord. XVII, Rule 1, proviso, The Civil Procedure Code.
24. *Sukhpal Singh* v. *Kalyan Singh*, AIR 1983 SC 146.
25. Ord. XVI, Rule 1 (1), The Civil Procedure Code.
26. S. 32, The Civil Procedure Code.
27. S. 314(1), Code of Criminal Procedure.
28. S. 314(2), Code of Criminal Procedure .
29. Ord. XVI, Rr. 3A, 3D, Civil Procedure Code.
30. Abdul Gaffur; *Delay in Criminal Trial*; Central India Law Quarterly; Vol. XV; 2002; p. 90.
31. Order IX, Rule-1, Civil Procedure Code.
32. Order VI, Rule-17, The Code of Civil Procedure.
33. Rule-17, Proviso (added by the amendment of the Code of Civil Procedure in 2002).
34. G.M. Dinkar, "*A Note On Laws Delay*", XXIII, (1) Indian Bar Review at 75 (1996).
35. *Supra* note 23, at p. 91.
36. *Supra* note 4, at p. 592.
37. 77th Report of Law Commission of India on '*Delays in Trial*', Dec. 1978.
38. Ord. XXI, rule-6, Code of Civil Procedure.
39. Ord. XXI, rule-26(1) Code of Civil Procedure: The court to which the decree has been sent for execution shall, upon sufficient cause being sown, stay the execution of such decree for a reasonable time to enable the judgment-debtor to apply to the court by which the decree was passed or to any other court having appellate jurisdiction in respect of the decree or the execution thereof, for an order to stay the execution or for any other order relating to the decree or execution which might have been made by such court of first instance or Appellate court.
40. 127th Report of the Law Commission of India (1988), Vol. III.
41. (2002) 4 SCC 247.
42. (2005) 6 SCC 344.
43. Figure was given by him while delivering lecture in the "All India Seminar on Access to Justice" held on 6th-8th April 2007.
44. *Ibid.*
45. AIR 1982 SC 149.
46. Nyaya Deep; Journal of NALSA; Extract from Speech delivered by Justice K.G. Balakrishnan at Society of Lincoln's Inn, London, p. 5.
47. Uphaar Fire Tragedy Case.

48. Art. 235 *inter alia* provides that the control over district courts and courts subordinate thereto including the posting and promotion of, and the grant of leave to, persons belonging to the judicial service of a state and inferior post of a district judge shall be vested in the High Court.
49. Journal of Indian Law Institute ; Vol. 48:1, 2006; p. 94.
50. Justice Arijit Prasayat, '*Judicial Independence and Accountability*'; NYAYA DEEP, Journal of NALSA; Vol. II, Oct., 2007; p. 46.
51. Justice B.N. Agarwal, "*Judicial Accountability*", AIR April 2008 (Journal Section); p. 50.
52. Sec. 4, Right to Information Act, 2005.
53. *Id.* Sec. 2(h).
54. Supra note-51; p. 52.
55. Report was submitted in 1996.
56. S.S. Siddiqi and Y. Abbasi "*Speeding up the Justice Delivery System with Special Reference to Procedural Reforms*", Published in Souvenir on 'All India Seminar on Judicial Reforms'.
57. A.R. Qureshi; "Court Vacations and Court Delays", published in AIR 1999 (Journal Section) p. 43.
58. Supra Note- 35, at p. 13.
59. *Ibid.*
60. Coutsey http://www.newindianexpress.com/thesundaystandard/Supreme-Sacrifice-for-Speedy-Justice/2013/12/29/article1970479.
61. AIR 1981 SC 298.
62. *S.P. Gupta* v. *Union of India*, AIR 1982 SC, 149.
63. AIR 1987 SC 1109.
64. (1992) 4 SCC 305.
65. R. Madhavi, '*Witness attack on Justice*'; JUSTITIA , Osmania University Law Journal; p. 86.
66. *Zahira Habibullah Sheikh and another* v. *State of Gujarat* (AIR 2006 SC 1367).
67. G.S. Shekhar; '*Witness Protection in Criminal Cases*'; The Frontline, September, 2005; p. 76.
68. *Id.*, at p. 77.
69. The difference between Arts.32 and 226 is that through Art.32 Supreme court can be approached for the enforcement of Fundamental rights only, while through Art. 226 High Courts can be approached not only for the enforcement of Fundamental rights but also for the enforcement of any other rights.
70. *The Academy Law Review;* Vol. 17, p. 59.
71. *Id.* at p. 60.

4

Mechanisms to Speed-up Justice Delivery System

1. Use of Alternative Dispute Resolution Techniques:
   - 1.1 Arbitration
   - 1.2 Mediation
   - 1.3 Conciliation
   - 1.4 Negotiation
   - 1.5 Counseling
   - 1.6 Lok Adalat
2. Other Relevant Measures:
   - 2.1 Fast Track Courts
   - 2.2 Plea Bargaining
   - 2.3 Use of Technology in Case Management
3. Recommendations of Various Commissions
4. Initiative Taken by the Supreme Court of India
5. Law Commission of India Report 2012 on Expeditious Investigation and Trial of Criminal Cases Against Influential Public Personalities
6. Conclusion

"Discourage litigation, persuade your neighbors to compromise whenever you can. Point out to them how the normal winner is often a loser in fees".

—Abraham Lincoln

"The speedy arm of justice was never Known to fail; The gaol supplied the gallows; the Gallows thinned the gaol, And sundry wise precautions the Sages of the law discreetly framed whereby they Aimed to keep the rogues in awe."

—John W. Smith

Peace is the *sine qua non* for development. Disputes and conflicts dissipate valuable time, effort and money of the society. It is of utmost importance that there should not be any conflict in the society. But in a realistic sense, this is not possible. So, the next best solution is that any conflict which raises its head is nipped in the bud. With the judicial system in most of the countries being burdened with cases, any new case takes a long time to be decided. And till the time the final decision comes, there is a state of uncertainty, which makes any activity almost impossible. Commerce, business, development work, administration, etc., all suffer because of time taken in resolving disputes through litigation.

To get out of this maze of litigation, Courts of most of the countries encourage alternative methods of dispute resolution. India has a long tradition and history of such methods being practiced in the society at grass roots level. These are called **Panchayat** and in the legal terminology these are called **arbitration.** These are widely used in India for resolution of disputes—both commercial and non-commercial. Other alternative methods being used are **Lok Adalat (People's Court),** where justice is dispensed summarily without too much emphasis on legal technicalities. Methods like negotiation, mediation and conciliation are being increasingly used to resolve disputes instead of going for litigation. There have been amendments recently in the procedural law of India to incorporate these methods so that people get justice in a speedy manner and there is lesser conflict in the society.[1]

The Constitution of India guarantees '**Right to Constitutional Remedies**'[2] as a fundamental right. The Government provides free legal aid to the needy. However, in a country of continental dimensions and with population more than a billion, it becomes very difficult to provide free legal aid to everyone. The **National Legal Services Authority (NALSA)** is trying to spread 'legal literacy' which is a step more than 'literacy'. People care about their rights much more when they are aware and are 'legal literates'. Efforts are also being done at provincial level. All these efforts seem to be a small drop in the ocean, but small drops make mighty oceans.

Mahatma Gandhi,[3] the father of the Nation, wrote in his autobiography about the role of law and lawyer:

> "I had learnt the practice of law. I had learnt to find out the better side of human nature, and to enter men's hearts. I realized that the true function of a lawyer was to unite parties fallen apart. The lesson was so indelibly burnt into me that the large part of my time during the twenty years of my practice as a lawyer was occupied in bringing about private compromises of hundreds of cases. I lost nothing thereby—not even of money, certainly not my soul."

Any conflict is like cancer. The sooner it is resolved the better for all the parties concerned in particular and the society in general. If it is not resolved at the earliest possible opportunity, it grows at a very fast pace and with time the effort required to resolve it increases exponentially as new issues emerge and conflicting situations galore. One dispute leads to another. Hence, it is essential to resolve the dispute the moment it raises its head. The method to achieve this goal must be agreeable to both the parties and it should achieve the goal of resolving the dispute speedily. This state of uncertainty and indecisiveness should be as brief as possible to avoid all psychological, physical and mental losses.[4]

The Constitution of India in its preamble has defined and declared the common goal for its citizens as "to secure to all the citizens of India, justice—social, economic and political; liberty; equality and fraternity". The eternal value of constitutionalism is the rule of law which has three facets, i.e. rule by law, rule under law and rule according to law. How to secure to all the citizens the justice which the constitution talks about is a big question being faced by the judiciary. The Courts dockets are overloaded and new cases are being filed every day. It is becoming humanly impossible to decide all these cases by the regular courts in a speedy manner. And, this is not the situation in India alone. This, unfortunately, is the situation in many countries of the world.[5]

With the evolution of modern States and sophisticated legal mechanisms, the Courts run on very formal processes and are presided over by trained adjudicators entrusted with the responsibilities of resolution of disputes on the part of the State. The seekers of justice approach the Courts of justice with pain and anguish in their hearts on having faced legal problems and having suffered physically or psychologically. They do not take the law into their own hands as they believe that they would get justice from the Courts at the end. It is the obligation of judiciary to deliver quick and inexpensive justice shorn of the complexities of procedure. However, the reality is that it takes a very long time to get justice through the established court system. Obviously, this leads to a search for alternative complementary and supplementary mechanism to the process of traditional Civil Court for inexpensive, expeditious and less cumbersome and less stressful resolution of disputes. But, the elements of judiciousness, fairness, quality and compassion cannot be allowed to be sacrificed at the altar of expeditious disposal. The hackneyed saying is that **'justice delayed is justice denied: justice cannot be hurried to be buried'**. The cases have to be "decided" and not just "disposed of". This creates the dilemma of providing speedy and true justice. This is easier said than done.

The Indian judiciary is held in very high esteem in all the developing as well as the developed countries of the world. However, there is a criticism that the Indian judiciary is unable to clear the backlog of cases. Available and relevant statistics would show that though the pendency of cases is always highlighted, what is never spoken of are the figures of annual filing and disposal. During the year 2001-04, on an average, the subordinate Courts have disposed of 13 million cases every year while the High Courts have disposed of 1.5 million cases per year. The fast Track Courts have disposed of 370.000 cases during the same period. The Supreme Court of India is disposing of about 50,000 cases per year.[6] As per a recent report published by the Supreme Court of India, the rate of disposal by S.C. from May 2008 to April, 2009 is 61.850 and from May, 2010 to April 2011, it is 79,621. If you see disposal of cases on 5 years basis, in five years (31.12.2005 to 31-12-2010) cases filed in S.C., H.Cs and subordinate courts were 11.16 cr. and the disposal was 10.77 crore.

The law Courts are confronted with four main problems:[7]

(a) The number of Courts and Judges in all grades are alarmingly inadequate;
(b) Increase in flow of cases in recent years due to multifarious Acts enacted by the Central and State Governments;
(c) The high cost involved in prosecuting or defending a case in a court of law, due to heavy Court-fee, lawyer's fee and incidental charges; and
(d) Delay in disposal of cases resulting in huge pendency in all the Courts.

These problems do not have an instant solution. For each problem, there are a number of reasons which need to be tackled; however, it requires a lot of time and will power on the part of the leaders of the nation to tackle the situation. Till the time it is done, the country has to move on. Disputes will keep emerging and if not resolved, they shall keep on piling making life difficult for everyone in the society.

In every civilization, and India is no exception, pursuit of justice is instinctive. It is an individual and societal instinct and every society strives to attain it through its legal system. The degree of perfection attained by a legal system may be measured by the extent to which it exists in good instinct for justice system to express itself and to find its fulfillment. Not every legal system succeeds in this goal. Sometimes a legal system fails to achieve its purpose because of defects and deficiencies in its substantive laws and sometimes mainly because of infirmities in its procedural rules. Fortunately, the judicial system in India is well organized with high level of integrity, and has been able to develop a system of ADR.[8]

1. USE OF ALTERNATIVE DISPUTE RESOLUTION

Alternative Dispute Resolution, as the name suggests, is an alternative to the traditional process of dispute resolution through courts. It refers to a set of practices and techniques to resolve disputes outside the courts. It is mostly a non-judicial means or procedure for the settlement of disputes. In its wider sense, the term refers to everything from facilitated settlement negotiations in which parties are encouraged to negotiate directly with each other prior to some other legal process, to arbitration systems of mini trial that look and feel very much like a court room processes. It is not intended to replace or supplant the courts of the land but is in addition to the traditional system. It is not an alternative to the court system in a restrictive sense. The need for public adjudication and normative judicial pronouncements on the momentous issues of the day is fundamental to the evolution of the laws of the land. ADR is necessary to complement and preserve this function of the courts. It has some instrumental and intrinsic functions. It is instrumental in so far as it enables amicable settlement of disputes through means which are not available generally to court. It is intrinsic because it enables the parties themselves to settle their disputes.[9]

Alternative Dispute Resolution mechanisms are in addition to courts and complement them. The traditional system of dispute resolution is afflicted with inordinate delays. Nowhere, however, does backlog and delay appear to be more accentuated than in modern-day India. ADR mechanisms play an important role in doing away with delays and congestion in courts. The Indian civil justice system serves the interests of a diverse and exploding population of the largest democracy and the seventh largest national market in the world. This formidable responsibility combined with the recent drive toward greater political accountability in the public administration and post-1991 market reforms places very greater pressure on the civil justice system. An estimated backlog of 28 million cases and reported delays in some urban areas of over twenty years, currently undermine the effective enforcement of the substantive civil and commercial rights. Backlog and delay have broad political and economic implications for the Indian society. If India fails to face and meet these challenges, it will not be able to realize fully its legal commitment to democratic and liberal economic policies. All agree that this crisis calls for the careful adaptation of workable solutions. In cases such as motor accident claims, the victim may require the compensation to be paid without delay in order to meet medical and other expenses. In matter such as these, alternative Dispute Resolution mechanisms can help victims obtain speedy relief. In addition to reducing the burden on the courts and proving speedy justice to people, Alternative Dispute Resolution mechanisms have been introduced and are being utilized for a number of other reasons also. Alternate Dispute Resolution mechanisms are relatively inexpensive in comparison with the ordinary legal process. These mechanisms, therefore, help litigants who are unable to meet the expenses involved in the ordinary process of dispute resolution through courts. Furthermore, ADR mechanism enhances the involvement of the community in the dispute resolution process.[10]

ADR mechanisms provide for more effective resolution of disputes as the parties are more involved in the process and the process is swift. Court processes that are traditionally practiced may not in every case provide the best approach towards the resolution of disputes. For instance, in the case of matrimonial disputes, which are sensitive in nature, involving both legal as well as emotional questions, the parties are not interested in winning or losing, but in reaching a solution. Inordinate delays that are a part of the ordinary legal process may emotionally affect the parties and cause frustration. The matter may be more effectively resolved, if it is not dealt with in a mechanical and technical manner. The procedures employed in Alternate Dispute Resolution are flexible and informal in contrast to the formal and rigid procedures followed in the ordinary process of dispute resolution in courts of law. These processes thus facilitate access to justice.

Definite Advantages of ADR[11]

(1) One of the foremost advantages of the Alternate Dispute Resolution process is that the dispute remains under the control of the parties themselves and any settlement entered into is their own and does not represent a dictate from an outsider. The process of Alternate Dispute Resolution be it mediation, negotiation or Lok Adalat implies a greater involvement of the disputing parties. The parties are actively involved in the process of dispute resolution and can, therefore, more effectively reach a settlement of the dispute.

(2) ADR processes, as mentioned earlier are not afflicted with the rigorous rules of procedure. No fixed set of rules are employed as such, be it in mediation or negotiation or even in Lok Adalats. In case of arbitration, however, the rules of arbitration institutions, which are fixed, are sometimes applied. In fact, the parties may meet and fix the procedures for themselves with the help of a mediator. It is much easier with more informal procedures to avoid the confusion involved in the usually stringent procedures.

(3) ADR processes are sometimes confidential and generally without prejudice. For instance, in the case of conciliation proceedings, the **Arbitration and Conciliation Act, 1996** specifically provides for the confidentiality of all matters relating to the proceedings. In arbitration agreements also, the parties themselves, often provide for confidentiality of the proceedings and the awards.[12]

(4) As ADR is not adversarial and aims for all sides ending up with at least a solution that is acceptable to all the parties involved, disputants can save face which again is important and indeed vital in relationship. Differences can be eased through this process and future relationship may be preserved and continued. Particularly in business relationships, the parties may wish to resolve their disputes amicably and carry on their trade in future. In such circumstances, ADR mechanisms such as mediation or arbitration may provide more effective means for the settlement of their disputes.

(5) Another advantage of Alternate Dispute Resolution mechanisms is that they can be used at any time either immediately after dispute arises or when dispute is pending with the court. In case of commercial relationships, the parties may agree at the time of entering into the contract to resort to any of the Alternate Dispute Resolution mechanisms in case a dispute arises. It can be terminated at any stage by any one of the disputants. In **Salem Advocate Bar Association, T.N.** *v.* **Union of India,**[13] Hon'ble Mr. Justice B.N. Kirpal the then Chief Justice of India, observed "In certain countries of the world, where ADR has been successful to that extent, that over 90 per cent of the cases are settled out of the court. There is a requirement that the parties to the suit must indicate the form of ADR which they would like to resort during the pendency of the trial of the suit".

(6) The parties are free to choose their mediator or arbitrator. This can lead to the appointment of persons who are familiar with the business or have other relevant expertise and can thus play a vital role in the effective resolution of the dispute.

ADR Strategies includes the following:

a) Arbitration
b) Negotiation
c) Mediation
d) Conciliation
e) Counseling
f) Lok Adalat

1.1 Arbitration

Arbitration is a process in which a neutral third party or parties render a decision based on the merits of the case. The parties to the arbitration have some control over the design of the arbitration process. In the Indian context, the scope of the rules for the arbitration process are set out broadly by the provisions of the **Arbitration and Conciliation Act 1996** and in the areas uncovered by the Statute the parties are free to design an arbitration process appropriate and relevant to their disputes. There is more flexibility in the arbitration process than in the traditional courts system as the parties can facilitate the creation of an arbitral process relevant to their disputes. Once the process is decided upon within the parameters of the Statute, the arbitrator assumes full control of the process. Among the advantages of the arbitration process are considerable saving in time and money as compared to a trial; the limited possibility for challenging the award which again contribute to the lower costs and finality of outcome; and greater participation by the parties than is the case in the courts/tribunal system.[14]

1.2 Negotiation

Negotiation in principle is any form of communication between two or more people for the purpose of arriving at a mutually agreeable solution. In negotiation the disputants may represent themselves or through negotiating agents. In this form of ADR, the disputants or their agents maintain control over the negotiation process. There are several techniques of negotiation such as competitive bargaining, cooperative bargaining and principled negotiation which are but different facets and styles of negotiations. In the **competitive bargaining** the negotiators are essentially concerned with substantive results and advocate extreme positions, create extravagant issues, mislead the other negotiators, create extravagant issues negotiator or even bluff in order to gain an advantage and to ascertain the other negotiator's bottom line. The dominant negotiator attempting the competitive bargaining technique makes concessions rarely and grudgingly.[15]

In **cooperative bargaining** both negotiators focus on building up a relationship of trust and cooperation. In this strategy the negotiators are prepared to make concession even on substantive issues as the endeavour is to preserve the relationship.

In **principled negotiations** the negotiator focus on the interest of each of the disputants, with the goal of creating satisfactory and elegant options for resolutions, which may be assessed by objective criteria.[16]

1.3 Mediations

The process of mediation aims to facilitate the development of a consensual solution by the disputing parties. The mediation process is overseen by a non-partisan third party- the Mediator. The authority of the mediator vests on the consent of the parties that he should facilitate their negotiations. The mediator has no independent decision-making power, jurisdiction or legitimacy beyond what is voluntarily offered by the parties themselves. This process, as is apparent, is in contrast to our adjudicative system where the court is an authoritative third party decision maker.[17]

Mediator employs several strategies, sub-strategies and techniques to encourage the parties to reach an agreement. Some times mediators generate objective criteria, viz., standards for determining fairness which are recognized and agreed by the parties to the dispute. These standards may not be the same as legal standards. For example, objective criteria may include industry or commercial practices which do not have legal recognition, but may be agreed upon as fair standards for resolution of disputes by the parties themselves. In some case the mediator assists the parties with specific provisions of a settlement arrangement. In any event the essence and effectiveness of mediation is in the ability to create conditions under which the parties will conclude a successful negotiation. World over the mediation process is now used in a wide range of conflicts such as family matters, major commercial and business disputes, personal injury suits, employment disputes, medical care disputes as well as conflicts having a public dimension such as environmental disputes, professional disciplinary proceedings and criminal prosecutions as well.[18]

Mediation like other ADR strategies has distinct advantages over the traditional court's/tribunal's format of dispute resolution. The advantages of ADR including mediation are the informality of the process, the ability of the process to focus on the disputing parties' interests and concern rather than exclusively on their legal rights; much greater involvement of the parties in the process; the essential confidentiality of the process and the high success rate.[19]

1.4 Conciliation

This is a process by which resolution of disputes is achieved by compromise or voluntary agreement. In contrast to arbitration, the conciliator does not render a binding award. The parties are free to accept or reject the recommendations of the conciliator. The conciliator is, in the Indian context, often a Government official whose report contains recommendations. The conciliation process is sometimes considered synonymous to mediation. There is however a difference. Where a third party is informally involved without a provision under any law, it is known as mediation. In other words, a non-statutory conciliation is what mediation is. However in effect and structure, conciliation and mediation are substantially identical strategies where a stranger to the dispute provides assistance to parties to a dispute. Both the conciliator and mediator are required to bring to the process of dispute resolution fairness, objectivity, neutrality, independence, and considerable expertise to facilitate a resolution of the conflict.[20]

1.5 Counseling

Counseling is the most important component of ADR. Lawyers should be trained as lawyer counselors. Counseling is a process that enables a person to sort out issues and reach decisions affecting his or her life. Although, counseling is often sought at times of change or crisis but it can also help us at any time of our lives. It involves talking with a person so as to help that person solve a problem or help create conditions that will cause the person to understand and improve his behaviour, character and values of life.

Stages in Legal Counseling

The various stages of legal counseling are:[21]

(a) *Fact Gathering*: The Lawyer-counselor has to first gather enough facts to form an accurate picture of the client's situation, facts as the client sees them and facts that the lawyer helps the client to see. The information that the lawyers gather depends on:

- The lawyer's approach;
- The client's initial impression of the lawyer and the place at which they work together;
- The initial feelings of the lawyer and client with regard to each other;
- The manner in which the lawyer goes after the information;
- The lawyer's perception of the facts as the client provides them; and
- The lawyer's understanding of the clients concerns, as these are placed in their broader context (the client's story and how the client sees the world).

(b) *Choice*: Choice is the direction that the clients determine to take as a result of counseling. The lawyer helps the client make up his mind. The client has to make a choice about what he wants to do or what course of action he has to follow.

(c) *Decisions*: The lawyer-counselor has to work with the client to come to a decision. The lawyer can suggest options, provide information (about law, the options available to the client as well as other pertinent information), identify moral concerns, predict consequences and represent the interest of persons who are not in the room, but will be affected by the decision. After a client has determined what decision he is going to take, he has to decide how he is going to carry out what he has chosen to do and what legal strategies can be used. The skills required in assisting and guiding the client to reach a decision include—interaction skills, skills involving cooperation, coordination, explanation, foresight and a sense of consequence.

According to **Richard Wallen,** there are four stages involved in the process of counseling. These are: Interview, Choice, Decision and Solution. The steps involved in reaching a solution are:[22]

A. Formulation
B. Producing proposals
C. Forecasting consequences

Role of the Counselor

The role of the counselor is basically to be there for the client. S/he does not analyze, criticize, agree, disagree, advice, and interpret verbally or non-verbally. The counselor should help and guide the parties and should not pass a judgment on them. S/he must remain objective throughout the process. A counselor should work as an information-giver, consultant and resource builder. S/he does give supportive expectant and validatory attention to the client to his/her words, tone of voice, posture, etc.

According to **Benjamin, P.I.**[23] although counselors sometimes have to ask questions but a few protective standards have to be adopted by them:

- The Counselor should be aware of the fact that s/he is asking questions.
- The Counselor should challenge the questions that s/he is about to ask.
- The Counselor should examine carefully the various kinds of questions available and types of questions s/he personally tends to use.
- The Counselor should consider alternatives to asking questions.
- The Counselor should be sensitive to the questions the client is asking, whether he is asking them outright or not.

1.6 Lok Adalat

"Sun shines in his full force, calendar shows it is Sunday. A public building, usually morose, is bustling with activities. Crowd appears unusual, room give the appearance of courts, there is process going on to reconcile the conflicts between the opposite parties, a judge-like man announces Rs. 13.5 lacs as compensation to the victim of motor accident. All are happy. Neither is there any loser nor any victor. Peace and love prevail over the conflict." This is not a still from any flick, but is a real life activity as the banner decorating the entrance gate rightly speaks of it as 'Lok Adalat'.

The concept of Lok Adalat (Peoples' Court) is an innovative Indian contribution to the jurisprudence. The institution of Lok Adalat in India, as the very name suggests, means People's Court. "Lok" stands for people and the vernacular meaning of the term "Adalat" is the Court. India has a long tradition and history of such methods being practiced in the society at grass roots level. These are called **Panchayat** and in the legal terminology, these are called arbitration. These are widely used in India for resolution of disputes both commercial and non-commercial. Other alternative methods being used are Lok Adalat (People's Court), where justice is dispensed summarily without too much emphasis on legal technicalities. It has been proved to be a very effective alternative to litigation. Lok Adalat is one of the fine and familiar forums which has been playing an important role in the settlement of disputes.[24]

The ancient concept of settlement of dispute through mediation, negotiation or arbitral process known as **"Peoples Court verdict"** or decision of **"Nyaya-Panch"** is conceptualized and institutionalized in the philosophy of Lok Adalat. Some people equate Lok Adalat to conciliation or mediation; some treat it with negotiations and arbitration. Those who find it different from all these, call it "Peoples Court". It involves people who are directly or indirectly affected by dispute resolution. The salient features of this form of dispute resolution are participation, accommodation fairness, expectation, voluntariness, neighbourliness, transparency, efficiency and lack of animosity.[25]

Lok Adalats have worked very well and satisfactorily in our country. Camp of Lok Adalat was started initially in Gujarat in March 1982 and now it has been extended throughout the country. The evolution of this movement was a part of the strategy to relieve heavy burden on the courts with pending cases. The reason to create such camps were only the pending cases and to give relief to the litigants who were in a queue to get justice. The first Lok Adalat was held on March 14, 1982 at Junagarh in Gujarat, the land of Mahatma Gandhi. Lok Adalats have been very successful in settlement of motor accident claim cases, matrimonial/family disputes, labour disputes, disputes relating to public services such as telephone, electricity, bank recovery cases and so on.[26]

Some statistics may give us a feeling of tremendous satisfaction and encouragement. Up to December **2007** more than 200,000 Lok Adalats have been held and therein more than **18 million** cases have been settled, half of which were motor accident claim cases. More than one billion US dollars were distributed by way compensation to those who had suffered accident and around 6.7 million persons have got benefit through legal aid and advice in the Lok Adalat. Between 2001 and 2002, a total of 104,728 Lok Adalats were conducted all across India and they disposed of more than 2.4 million cases.

Benefits of Lok Adalat

The benefit that litigants derive through the Lok Adalat is many. **Firstly**, there is no Court fee and even if the case is already filed in the regular Court, the fee paid will be refunded if the dispute is settled at the Lok Adalat.

Secondly, there is no strict application of the procedural laws and the Evidence Act while assessing the merits of the claim by Lok Adalat. The parties to the disputes though represented by their advocate can interact with the Lok Adalat judge directly and explain their stand in the dispute, which is not possible in a regular court of law.

Thirdly, disputes can be brought before the Lok Adalat directly instead of going to a regular court first and then to the Lok Adalat.

Fourthly, the decision of the Lok Adalat is binding on the parties to the dispute and its order is capable of execution through legal process. No appeal lies against the order of the Lok Adalat whereas in the regular law courts there is always a scope to appeal to the higher forum against the decision of the trial court, which causes delay in the final settlement of the dispute. The reason being that in a regular court, decision is that of the court but in Lok Adalat it is mutual settlement and hence there is no cause for appeal. In every respect the scheme of Lok Adalat is a boon to the litigant public where they can get their disputes settled fast and free of cost.[27]

The system has received laurels from the parties involved in particular and the public and legal functionaries, in general. It also helps in emergence of jurisprudence of peace in the larger interest of justice and wider sections of society. Its process is voluntary and works on the principle that both parties to the disputes are willing to sort out their disputes by amicable solutions. Through this mechanism, disputes can be settled in a simpler, quicker and cost-effective way at all the three stages, i.e. pre-litigation, pending litigation and post-litigation.

Procedure at Lok Adalat

The procedure followed at the Lok Adalat is very simple and shorn of almost all legal formalism and rituals. The Lok Adalat is presided over by a sitting or retired judicial officer as the **Chairman**, with **two other members**, usually **a lawyer** and **a social worker**. It is revealed by experience that in Lok Adalat, it is easier to settle money claims since in most of such cases the quantum alone may be in dispute. Thus, the motor accident compensation claim assets are brought before the Lok Adalat and a number of cases are disposed of in each Lok Adalat. One important condition is that both the parties in dispute should agree for settlement through Lok Adalat and abide by its decision.[28]

A Lok Adalat has the jurisdiction to settle, by way of effecting compromise between the parties, any matter which may be pending before any Court as well as matters at pre-litigative stage i.e. disputes which have not yet been formally instituted in any Court of Law. Such matters may be civil or criminal in nature, but any matter relating to an offence not compoundable under any law cannot be decided by the Lok Adalat even if the parties involved therein agree to settle the same. Lok Adalats can take cognizance of matters involving not only those persons who are entitled to avail free legal services but of all other persons also, be they women, men, or children and even institutions.[29]

Anyone, or more of the parties to a dispute can move an application to the Court where their matter may be pending, or even at pre-litigative stage, for such matter being taken up by the Lok Adalat. In such a situation , the Lok Adalat Bench constituted for the purpose shall attempt to resolve the dispute by helping the parties to arrive at an amicable solution and once it is successful in doing so, the award passed by it shall be final which has as much force as a decree of a Civil Court obtained after due contest.

Legislation pertaining to Lok Adalat

Ever since 1987, Lok Adalats have been given statutory recognition. The **Legal Services Authorities Act, 1987**, pursuant to the constitutional mandate in **Article 39-A** of the Constitution of India,[30] contains various provisions for settlement of disputes through Lok Adalat. Thus, the ancient concept of Lok Adalat has, now got a statutory basis. It is an Act to constitute legal services authorities to provide free and competent legal services to the weaker sections of the society to ensure that opportunities for securing justice are not denied to any citizen by reason of economic or other disabilities and to organize Lok Adalats to secure that the operation of the legal system promotes justice on a basis of equal opportunity to everybody. In 2002, Indian Parliament amended the Legal Services Authorities Act, 1987 requiring establishment of permanent Lok Adalats for public utility services.

The Legal Services Authorities Act, 1987 as amended in 2002 provides for setting up of a "**Permanent Lok Adalat**" which can be approached by any party to a dispute involving "public utility services" which have been defined in the Act (as amended) to include transport services for the carriage of passengers or goods by air, road or water; postal, telegraph or telephone services; insurance service and also services in hospital or dispensary supply of power, light or water to the public conservancy or sanitation. Any civil dispute with a public utility service and where the value of the property in dispute does not exceed Rupees one million (about US $ 2200); or any criminal dispute which does not involve an offence not compoundable under any law, can be taken up in the Permanent Lok Adalat.[31]

An important feature of this amendment is that after an application is made to the Permanent Lok Adalat, no party to that application can invoke jurisdiction of any Court in the same dispute. Such disputes involving public utility services shall be attempted to be settled by the Permanent Lok Adalat by way of conciliation and failing that, on merit, and in doing so the Permanent Lok Adalat shall be guided by the principles of natural justice, objective fair play, equity and other principles of justice without being bound by the Code of Civil Procedure and the Indian Evidence Act.[32]

Besides the Legal Services Authorities Act, there have been several other changes in the law in recent times and one of the most important being the amendment in Code of Civil Procedure. **Section 89** of the **Code of Civil Procedure as amended in 2002** has opened the scope for introduction of conciliation, mediation and pre-trial settlement methodologies. Once the provision will be implemented in its letter and spirit, this would drastically bring down the pendency of cases by accelerating disposal of such cases outside the Court. In California, U.S., where the systems of mediation, conciliation and pre-trial settlement have been introduced only two decades ago, it has been found that 94% of cases are referred for settlement through one or the other of the ADR systems and 46% of such cases are settled without contest. The result is that California has been able to achieve in civil matters the goal of final decision within a period of less than 2 years from the date of institution. The mediators and conciliators shall have to be trained so as to acquire professional expertise in the art of mediation and conciliation in India.[33]

The Constitutional validity of amendments made to **Section 89** of the **Code of Civil Procedure** incorporating Alternative Disputes Resolution methods have been upheld by the Supreme Court of India in a recently decided case.[34]

Some of the relevant Sections from the Legal Services Authority Act, 1987 are quoted as under:

Section 19

1. Central, State, District and Taluk Legal Services Authority has been created who are responsible for organizing Lok Adalats.
2. Conciliators for Lok Adalat comprise the following :
   (a) A sitting or retired judicial officer.
   (b) Other persons of repute as may be prescribed by the State Government in consultation with the Chief Justice of High Court.

Section 20: Reference of Cases

Cases can be referred for consideration of Lok Adalat as under:

1. By consent of both the parties to the disputes.
2. One of the parties makes an application for reference.
3. Where the Court is satisfied that the matter is an appropriate one to be taken cognizance by the Lok Adalat.
4. Compromise settlement shall be guided by the principles of justice, equity, fair play and other legal principles.
5. Where no compromise has been arrived at through conciliation, the matter shall be returned to the concerned Court for disposal in accordance with Law.

Section 21

After the agreement is arrived by the consent of the parties, the conciliators pass award. The matter need not be referred to the concerned Court for consent decree.

The Act provisions envisage as under:

1. Every award of Lok Adalat shall be deemed as decree of Civil Court.
2. Every award made by the Lok Adalat shall be final and binding on all the parties to the dispute.
3. No appeal shall lie from the award of Lok Adalat.

Section 22

Every proceedings of the Lok Adalat shall be deemed to be judicial proceedings for the purpose of:

(i) Summoning of Witnesses.
(ii) Discovery of documents.
(iii) Reception of evidence.
(iv) Requisitioning of Public record.[35]

Finality of Lok Adalat Award

One issue that often raises its head is the finality of the award of the Lok Adalat. During the Lok Adalat, the parties agree to abide by the decision of the judge of the Lok Adalat. However, it is often seen that later the same order is challenged on several grounds. In one of the recent decisions, the Supreme Court of India has once again laid to rest all such doubts. In unequivocal terms, the court has held that award of the Lok Adalat is as good as the decree of a Court. The award of the Lok Adalat is fictionally deemed to be decree of Court and therefore the Courts have all the powers in relation thereto as it has in relation to a decree passed by itself. This includes the powers to extend time in appropriate cases. The award passed by the Lok Adalat is the decision of the Court itself though arrived at by the simpler method of conciliation instead of the process of arguments in Court.[36] In *P.T Thomas* v. *Thomas Job*[37] the Supreme Court held that an award given of the Lok Adalat made with the consent of the parties is not appealable under Sec. 96(3) of the Code of Civil Procedure.

Consent of Parties

The most important factor to be considered while deciding the cases at the Lok Adalat is the consent of both the parties. It cannot be forced on any party that the matter has to be decided by the Lok Adalat and then any party cannot walk away from the decision of the Lok Adalat. In several instances, the Supreme Court has held that if there was no consent, the award of the Lok Adalat is not executable and also if the parties fail to agree to get the dispute resolved through Lok Adalat, the regular litigation process remains open for the contesting parties.[38]

A compromise is always bilateral and means mutual adjustment. "Settlement" is termination of legal proceedings by mutual consent.

If no compromise or settlement is or could be arrived at, the Lok Adalat can pass no order.

2. OTHER RELEVANT MEASURES

2.1 Fast Track Courts

Setting up of fast Track Courts is yet another mode of speeding up the justice delivery system in India. Fast Track Courts had originally been meant for reducing pendency in criminal matters, but with the passage of time the same have to be introduced to reduce pendency in civil matters also. Around **2500 Fast Track Courts** were functional as on **March 2007**. Due to the effectiveness of the Fast Track Courts, the Central Government has also approved the continuation of the existing Fast Track Courts and that at least a 1000 more Fast Track Courts shall become functional by the end of 2008. The objective behind the setting up of such courts was mainly the discharge of under-trials languishing in jails for petty offences. There are around 1.80 lakh such cases all over the country. This also addresses a serious human rights issue as the right to a speedy trial has been held to be a fundamental right by the Apex Court in a number of judgments. Further the cost effectiveness of the mechanism also helps in reducing the jail expenditure, which may then be utilized for other purposes.[39] Former Law and Justice Minister Kapil Sibal said in the Lok Sabha that a total of 3,292,785 cases were disposed of by the 1,192 Fast Track courts till March 2011. He said there are more than 32 million pending cases in hight courts and subordinate court across the country. (Published 23-12-13. *(The Indian Express)*

Fast Track Courts have various problems in their operation:

(a) Precise form and contents needs to be clearly defined.

(b) Problem of manpower and lack of attention to such courts by practicing lawyers, etc.

(c) The legal sanctity of Fast Track Courts have also been challenged on the ground that they do not form part of the judiciary and that their decisions are, therefore, not binding or final.

(d) There has been a criticism that "**Justice hurried is justice buried**".[40]

2.2 Plea Bargaining

Various strategies and tools have been used in various

jurisdictions to lessen the burden of trials and ensure speedy disposal of cases. One such strategy is Plea Bargaining, which is presently in place in a number of countries including India. **The Code of Criminal Procedure (Amendment) Act, 2005** has introduced the concept of plea bargaining in India. It affords all members of the community to resolve cases without going to trial. The accused, the victim and the prosecution settle the outcome between themselves and the judge gives his approval. It is hoped that ADR in this context will be able to bring the accused and the victims of the crime together and help them to reach a mutual satisfactory disposition that will both compensate the victim and re-establish contact between the accused and the victim.

There is no perfect or simple definition of 'Plea Bargaining'. As the term implies, Plea Bargaining involves an active negotiation process whereby offender is allowed to confess his guilt in court if he so desires, in exchange of lighter punishment that would have been fixed for such offence. Black's Law Dictionary defines it as: "the process whereby the accused and the prosecutor in a criminal case work out a mutually satisfactory disposition of the case subject to court approval. It usually involves the defendants pleading guilty to a lesser offence or to only one or some of the counts of a multi-count indictment in return for a lighter sentence than that possible for the graver charge".[41]

Plea Bargaining can mainly be classified into three types: (1) Charge Bargaining; (2) Sentence Bargaining and (3) Fact Bargaining; Each type involves implied sentence reductions but differs in the ways of achieving those reductions. The **charge bargaining** is such bargain in which a defendant pleads guilty to reduced charge. Second type is **sentence bargaining** which involves assurance of lighter or alternative sentences in return for a defendants pleading guilty. The third type of plea bargaining is the **fact bargaining** and is least used in which negotiation involves an admission to certain facts in return for an agreement not to introduce certain other facts into evidence. [42]

Plea bargaining is the primary apparatus through which judges, public prosecutors, accused, investigating officers and victim cooperate and work together towards their individual and collective goals. In most cases, plea bargaining is to avoid the uncertainty of the trial and minimize the risk of undesirable results for either side.

Plea Bargaining and Indian Judiciary

The statement of objects and reasons, *inter alia*, mentions that, the disposal of criminal trials in the courts takes considerable time and that in many cases trials do not commence for as long as three to five years after the accused was remitted to judicial custody. Though not recognized by the criminal jurisprudence, it is seen as an alternative method to deal with the huge arrears of criminal cases. The bill attracted enormous public debate. Critics said it is not recognized and against public policy under our criminal justice system.[43]

The Supreme Court has also time and again blasted the concept of plea bargaining saying that negotiation in criminal cases is not permissible. More recently in *State of Uttar Pradesh* v. *Chandrika*[44] the court held that, mere acceptance or admission of guilt should not be a ground for reduction of sentence. Nor can the accused bargain with the court that as he is pleading guilty and the sentence be reduced. Despite this huge hue and cry, the government found it acceptable and finally section 265-A to 265-L have added in the Code of Criminal Procedure so as to provide for raising the plea bargaining in certain types of criminal cases.

While commenting on this aspect, the division bench of the Gujarat High Court observed in *State of Gujarat* v. *Natwar Harchanji Thakor*[45] that, the very object of law is to provide easy, cheap and expeditious justice by resolution of disputes, including the trial of criminal cases and considering the present realistic profile of the pendency and delay in disposal in the administration of law and justice, fundamental reforms are inevitable. There should not be anything static. It can thus be said that it is really a measure and redressal and it shall add a new dimension in the realm of judicial reforms.

The Supreme Court of India has examined the concept of plea bargaining in the case of *Murlidhar Meghraj Loyat* v. *State of Maharashtra*[46] and *Kasambhai* v. *State of Gujarat*[47]. In Kasambhai's case, the Supreme Court resisted a plea of guilt based on plea bargaining, as it would be opposed to public policy, if an accused were to be convicted by inducing him to plead guilty, by holding out a light sentence as an allurement.

In the case of *Murlidhar Meghraj Loyat* v. *State of Maharashtra*[48], the Supreme Court observed as under: "we are free to confess to a hunch that the appellants had hastened with their pleas of guilty hopefully, induced by an informal, tripartite understanding of light sentence in lieu of nolo contendere stance. Many economic offenders resort to practices the Americans call 'plea bargain', 'plea negotiation', 'trading out' and 'compromise in criminal cases' and the trial magistrate drowned by a docket burden nods assent to the sub rosa anteroom settlement. It is idle to speculate on the virtue of negotiated settlements of criminal cases, as obtained in the United States but in our jurisdiction, especially in the area of dangerous economic crimes and food offences, this practice intrudes on society's interests by opposing society's decision expressed through predetermined legislative fixation of minimum sentences and by subtly subverting the mandate of the law".[49]

In civil cases we find compromises actually encouraged as a more satisfactory method of settling disputes between individuals than an actual trial. However, if the dispute... finds itself in the field of criminal law, "law enforcement" repudiates the idea of compromise as immoral, or at best a necessary evil. The "state" can never compromise. It must "enforce the law." Therefore, open methods of compromise are impossible.

Therefore, the purpose of plea bargaining is also to see that the criminals who admit their guilt and repent upon, a lenient view should be taken while awarding punishment to them. But the legislature has not thought it proper to give right to the individual to compound any offence and every offence in which loss to individual is also involved. When a person goes to the extent of opening fake account, putting fake signatures and getting cheques encashed on the basis of forged signatures, this shows his criminal bent of mind. If he really repents, he must undergo some punishment for his crime committed and the sufferance which he made to the society.

Considering the view of the Supreme Court in the above cases, it is quite evident that the term 'plea bargaining' existed since a long time. Though the judiciary did not find it necessary to recognize it then, however, now it has got the recognition and is being implemented as well. The importance of this doctrine has been well explained by the Indian judiciary.

Anatomy of Concept of Plea Bargaining

Apart from the provision of purporting speedy trials, a very significant merit of the concept of plea bargaining is that it involves both the accused and the victim in the whole process of the trial. It does not allow the victim to question the witnesses and challenge their statements from time to time. The onus of proof also lies with the prosecution, while the accused is considered to be innocent till the judgment is pronounced[50].

Finally, it reduces arrears and pendency in the system by diverting a large number of crimes for alternative settlement without trial under control of the court to ensure fairness in the process and avoid fraud and coercion from either side[51].

Moreover, **speedy trial** is a right of the accused that flows from the Constitution of India, Art. 21 as held by the Supreme Court. If the accused is acquitted after such long delay, one may envisage the unnecessary suffering he was subjected to. Many times such inordinate delay contributes to acquittal of guilty persons either because the evidence is lost or because of lapse of time, or due to other such factors. Whatever may be the reason, it is justice that becomes a casualty. What needs to be realized is that the quality of justice suffers not only when an innocent person is convicted or a guilty one is acquitted, but also when there is enormous delay in case proceedings[52]. Thus, there is an inbuilt safety mechanism to guard against inducement or threat.

The reasons for plea bargaining by either side may be several and are as follows:

For Accused: The Principal benefit of Plea Bargaining for most of the accuses is to receive a lighter sentence for a less severe charge than what might result from taking the case to trial and losing. There may be other benefits as well, such as:

(a) Getting out of jail;
(b) Resolving the matter quickly;
(c) Having fewer or less serious offences on one's record;
(d) Avoiding hassles of finding a good lawyer for contesting the trial;
(e) Avoiding publicity.[53]

For Judges and Prosecutors

Crowded calendars and over-burdened prisons provide powerful incentive to many judges and prosecutors. Plea Bargaining helps Courts and prosecutors manage caseloads. Judges often reason that using Plea Bargains to process out offenders allows judges to preside over efficient trials and to minimize the risk of rulings being overturned on appeal.[54]

For Victim

Plea Bargaining has canvassed 'victim-oriented reform' to the criminal justice administration. For the first time, a system of taking care of the interests of the victim has been introduced. It provides greater respect and consideration towards victim and their rights. It does so by giving greater choices to them in satisfactory disposition of the case and by providing a compulsory composition.[55]

2.3 Use of Technology in Case Management

Case Management through the use of technology is yet another means of curtailing delays in disposal of cases. Case Management can be defined as a judicial process which increases judicial control over (i) the identification of substantive issues, (ii) the exploration of utilizing ADR, and (iii) the time required to complete the procedural steps of a civil litigation. Case management, as a device, should be put into practice whenever and wherever it is feasible throughout the life of a case, the object being to save the maximum avoidable time of the judges and make it available to the judges to use it. Case Management has become an important job activity in the legal arena when we have to wade through huge paperwork in a time bound program. The benefits that the user could get by the application of technology in case management is: enhanced Flexibility, increase in productivity, improvement in litigant services, optimizing profits and reducing costs. This can indeed be achieved if the technology can define workflows to meet specific requirements; specify procedures including automatic updates of key dates and reminders to lawyer diaries; create screen layouts for the input and display of information, design documents in word processing system; process multiple task simultaneously on a single matter and electronically store documents with easy and precise retrieval capacity.[56]

Case Management refers to control of the movement of cases through a court or a method of managing cases within the litigation process. Lawyers generally need 'Case Management Software' to effectively manage their caseloads. With reference to a court, it is a sort of court process that allows a judge to monitor and manage the progress of a case as it moves through the system.[57]

The basic goals of any case management from the point of view of Court are:[58]

1. To reduce unnecessary delay in reaching a final determination of a case;
2. To reduce the costs of those involved in the case;
3. To encourage people involved in litigation to have a direct part in finding mutually satisfactory solutions;
4. To give the courts a wider power to decide cases or issues at an early stage without full trial;
5. To suggest the use of Alternative Dispute Resolution (ADR) where that is likely to be beneficial.

Case Management Software

For a better management of cases it is *sine qua non* to use case management software that consists of a database that is designed for lawyers and law firm staff to easily manage all the information.

Uses of CMS

Following are the uses of CMS:

(i) Relodex

"Relodex" in western parlance is a sort of folder that contains the name, address, phone number and other pertinent information of key contacts. Relodex include information of clients, interested parties, other lawyers, judges, and just about everyone else with which the lawyer/law firm has contact. All the constituents of firm are hooked by a password with the CMS. The moment there is a change in Relodex, it is available to everybody in the firm. Meaning thereby, there is no more looking in the paper file to find the client's phone numbers other pertinent information. Everything is available in the Relodex.[59]

(ii) Case/Matter Database

The next CMS function is to open the case or matter. Understanding how a new matter is created is key to understanding information flow in the firm/law department. In Law firms/Law departments, various pieces of the case information pass through many hands in different formats, e.g. paper form, handwritten or typed information, multiple document form, papers presented at trial court, appellate Court, Court of revision, etc. All these form a part of case database. This will be important in getting information about a case, list of witnesses, their statements, opposing counsels, etc.

(iii) Case Calendar

Next on the list of CMS functions is the calendar system. All the law firms maintain a case diary at trial court levels. High Court or Supreme Court providing for individual lawyer cause list. Well but they do not provide who is to file what? What is to be done next? Microsoft Outlook provide for these facilities. But they are not CMS by themselves. So the CMS should be able to provide for the calendaring facility as well. What if you could "assign" a list of critical dates to one key date? For example, a trial date is set. All you have to do is to schedule the trial date and time and a list of ticklers, deadlines, and appointments are automatically calendered for you. If the trial date changes, you simply change the key date and all assigned ticklers are automatically changed with it, taking into account holidays and weekends. This is called "rules based" calendaring and is a part of many of the Case Management Systems.[60]

(iv) Case Diary

During the hearing of a case, lawyers plead so many things in court but some of them don't become a matter of record; it is a matter of memory of the judge and the opposing party lawyer. How if we could simply encapsulate all this information in one go. A lawyer say: "I assure you that I will file my counter within a week. My steno was sick and I could not get the dictation to present the memo to the court" (In a case where counter affidavit has not been filed since 6 months). This becomes a part of case diary and the dictating machine records these words into the CMS like this:

"Court Name ....
Court No. 4
Item No. 9
Date: DD.MM.YYYY: Time 12.22 p.m.
Mr. X versus Mr. Y.

Advocate Shah – "I assure you that I will file my counter within a week. My steno was sick and I could not get the dictation to present the memo to the court"

Judge – "And you are granted this adjournment on your assurance that you will not seek any further time. Your client has already taken 6 months".

Advocate Joshi – "Your Honor! I hope this is the last chance or else we close his right to file a counter".

They do not form part of case records, but a sort of case diary monitoring the conduct of parties during the case. Yes, this makes every word concerning case, recordable and we make everybody responsible for what they said or did during the case.[61]

The case diary is a key component in a case management system. The attorney will use this function more than any other feature because it becomes the centre for case information and communications. This will constantly push up a lawyer to finish work in-time and meet with deadlines rather than failing them.

(v) Document Generation

Just think of all those events that take place in a case. We start from trial Court. In a civil case, for instance, a suit is instituted, written statement filed, list of witnesses, list of exhibits (documents admitted to evidence), list of documents not admitted, statements by experts, witnesses, plaintiff, defendant, etc. This is then supplemented by various papers those are created during appeals, revisions, reviews and other rounds of litigations. What if we could simply connect them with hyperlinks? Click on one document and get another. Read into the documents and relate all documents giving same message in one group. Document Review process and concept searching, all in one place, giving out all relevant documents at the push of a button. Same set of documents are available to all the parties and to the court from same data base.

The CMS is automatically integrated with your Word Processor; you need to enter data once and that is updated as and when entered. So it is seen that by using a CMS, the legal profession can change from a "word processing centric" environment to a "case management centric" environment. That is, the Case Management System is the main System on the computer desktop—not the Word Processor. Everything happens from within the Case Management System.

3. SUGGESTIONS FOR REFORM GIVEN BY VARIOUS COMMISSIONS

It is of paramount importance to reform the problem of delays at the earliest and provide justice to citizens of this country in a reasonable time. It is imperative so that the faith of the society in the justice delivery system can be maintained in a country like ours where people consider judges only next to God. So keeping in mind such things, various commissions and committees have, from time to time, came forward with their suggestions for tackling the mounting arrears of cases:

(a) Parliamentary Standing Committee on Home Affairs

Law Reform is a vast and complex topic. It embraces legislative reforms, reforms of the judicial system and most importantly reforming the mindsets of the Judges, the Lawyers and the Legislators. Financial constraints are a major fetter on wide ranging reforms. There is a plethora of unimplemented recommendations and reports gathering dust. Why? Because for the executive and the politician it is a low-priority enterprise with no vote catching potential. All over the world and among the young, there is spirit of questioning. Every institution is under scrutiny. The citizen demands, particularly in a democratic country like ours, that the legal and judicial system must reform and justify its existence by serving the community. The God-like mystique of the judiciary wearing impressive judicial robes is fast dissolving. Our legal and judicial system has to earn the respect of the community every year and every day or else suffer by comparison with the systems of other countries.

The **85th Report of the Parliamentary Standing Committee on Home Affairs** on **"Law's Delays: Arrears in Courts"**[62] has come out with alarming figures. It estimates that 24 million cases are pending in different courts all over the country. Some of them are pending since 1950. The judge-population ratio is 10.5 Judges for every 10 lakh citizens. In contrast, there are 107 Judges in the USA for 10 lakh citizens. In India only 0.2 percent of the GNP is spent on the judiciary. The High Courts have become the biggest bottle-necks in the judicial hierarchy with arrears of 8 lakhs in Allahabad, 6.5 lakhs in Madras, 3.08 lacs in Kerala and 2.4 lakhs in Bombay. Parliamentary Standing Committee on Home Affairs in its Eighty-fifth Report deliberated on a variety of topics of judicial reforms and found that there is immense scope and wide ambit of judicial Reforms and it was necessary to identify specific problem areas. The issues which arose for the Committee's deliberations, included, *inter alia*:

(i) Vacancies of Judges;

(ii) Pendency of cases in courts;
(iii) Specific action plans to tackle them;
(iv) Centrally sponsored schemes for infrastructural development of the judiciary;
(v) Need for amendment in the Memorandum of Procedure of Appointment of Judges of Supreme Court and High Courts;
(vi) Improvement in the quality of judgments and the need to tune our legal system to the post-WTO and the international patent regime;
(vii) Increasing the sanctioned strength of Judges of High Courts and Subordinate Courts;
(viii) Setting up of Benches of Supreme Court and High Courts;
(ix) Setting up of Tribunals to decide on disputes relating to matrimony, education, election petitions, and company matters, etc.;
(x) Increase the age of retirement of High Court and Supreme Court Judges;
(xi) Provisions of adjournments;
(xii) Provision of loans for young lawyers for libraries and computers;
(xiii) Use of retired judicial human resource to dispose of pending cases;
(xiv) Procedural reforms to curb delays;
(xv) Providing modern infrastructural facilities up to the subordinate courts;
(xvi) Alternative Dispute Resolution Mechanism;
(xvii) Introduction of Case Management System in the Courts;
(xviii) Classification, categorization and bunching of cases.

It was felt that to remove the bottlenecks arising out of the inherent deficiencies in law which results in the law's delays and to accelerate the disposal of cases, there is need to amend the existing statutes, i.e. the High Court Acts and Rules, Civil Procedure Code, Criminal Procedure Code, India Evidence Act and other procedural laws. It is also imperative to augment the strength of courts to provide them full physical and functional facilities, institution of alternative modes of disposal and provide modern information technology to courts. The Law Commission of India in its 154th

Report (1996) had already made a number of recommendations for speedy disposal of criminal cases.

The Committee requested the Ministry of Home Affairs to apprise it on the status of implementation of the recommendations. The ministry informed the Sub-committee that the report was referred to all the State Governments/Union Territory Administrations for their views/comments as the Criminal Law and Criminal Procedure are on the Concurrent List of the Seventh Schedule to the Constitution of India and Criminal Laws are administered by the State Governments. The views of the State Governments may be summed up as follows:

(i) Most of the States appreciated the recommendations of the Law Commission contained in its 154th Report on the Code of Criminal Procedure, 1973. Some of the States have set-up Committees to consider the implications of the Law Commission's Report.

(ii) On the point of Separate Investigating Agency, while the States commended the idea behind the proposal but they expressed apprehensions as to its practicability on account of financial implications.

(iii) Some States expressed the view that the provisions relating to anticipatory bail should be restricted in its application. There should be no bar to arrest the person by the police during the pendency of the application for anticipatory bail. After charge sheet is filed, anticipatory bail should not be granted.

(iv) There was general agreement that many more offences be made compoundable.

(v) The concept of Plea Bargaining found favour with most of the States (Now Plea Bargaining has been introduced by the Criminal Law Amendment Act of 2005).

(vi) As regards victimology, control of victimization and protection of victims of crimes, there was general agreements, but it was considered necessary that nature of the crime, victim and amount of compensation for each offence should be duly considered and laid down.

(vii) Some States expressed the view that for minor offences of regulatory nature, there need not be strict separation between the Judiciary and the Executive. The Executive Magistrates may be given the power to try and dispose them off. Such offences are generally victimless crimes. One state suggested that cases of Maintenance may be given to Executive Magistrates, for granting interim relief after a short inquiry and thereafter the case may be passed on to the Judicial Magistrate concerned.

(viii) One State suggested that **Section 9 of the Cr.P.C.** be amended on the lines of Section 11 thereof with a view to enable the State government to establish special courts of Sessions Judges. It further suggested that in cases triable by Sessions Court, there should not be any committal proceeding of cases triable by them.

(ix) The concept of Nyaya Panchayat was welcomed by most of the States.

(x) Almost all the States agreed on the concept of establishing independent Directorate of Prosecution. Most of them already have them. States were also of the view that the Directorate of Prosecution should be neither under the police nor under the Home Department. It should only be under the Department of Law to ensure its independence.

(xi) One State noting that the subject-matter of Penal Law and Criminal Procedure is in the Concurrent List, expressed the view that there need not be uniform law for the whole country. States may have their own amendments, suitable to their needs.

(b) National Commission to Review the Working of the Constitution (NCRWC)

The National Commission to Review the Working of the Constitution which was set-up by the Government of India in 2002 had also given various suggestions for better management of court work, computerization of court system and increased settlements by Lok Adalats, etc. to bring down the arrears. The following suggestions were given by the NCRWC :

(1) In the matter of appointment of Judges of the Supreme Court, it would be worthwhile to have a participatory mode with the participation of both the Executive and the Judiciary in making recommendations. The composition of the Collegium gives due importance to and provides for the effective participation of both the Executive and the judicial wings of the State as an integrated scheme for the machinery for appointment of judges. *A National Judicial*

Commission under the Constitution should be established. The National Judicial Commission for appointment of judges of the Supreme Court shall comprise of:

(i)	The Chief Justice of India	: Chairman
(ii)	Two senior most Judges of the Supreme Court	: Member
(iii)	The Union Minister for Law and Justice	: Member
(iv)	One eminent person nominated by the President after consulting the Chief Justice of India	: Member

The establishment of a National Judicial Commission and its composition are to be treated as integral in view of the need to preserve the independence of the judiciary.[63]

(2) A committee comprising the Chief Justice of India and two senior-most Judges of the Supreme Court will comprise the committee of the National Judicial Commission exclusively empowered to examine complaints of deviant behaviour of all kinds and complaints of misbehaviour and incapacity against judges of the Supreme Court and the High Courts. If the committee finds that the matter is serious enough to call for a fuller investigation or inquiry, it shall refer the matter for a full inquiry to the committee [constituted under the Judges' (Inquiry) Act, 1968]. The committee under the Judges Inquiry Act shall be a permanent committee with a fixed tenure with composition indicated in the said Act and not one that is constituted *ad-hoc* for a particular case or from case to case, as is the present position under section 3(2) of the Act. The tenure of the inquiry committee shall be for a period of four years and to be re-constituted every four years. The President in consultation with the Chief Justice of India shall constitute the inquiry committee. The inquiry committee shall inquire into and report on the allegation against the Judge in accordance with the procedure prescribed by the said Act, i.e. in accordance with the sub-sections (3) to (8) of Section 3 and sub-section (1) of Section 4 of the said Act and submit their report to the Chief Justice of India, who

shall place before a committee of seven senior-most Judges of the Supreme Court. The Committee of seven Judges shall take a decision as to – whether (a) findings of the inquiry committee are proper; and (b) any charge or charges are established against the judge and if so, whether the charges held proved are so serious as to call for his removal (i.e. proved misbehaviour) or whether it should be sufficient to administer a warning to him and/or make other directions with respect to allotment of work to him by the concerned Chief Justice or to transfer him to some other court (i.e. deviant behaviour not amounting to misbehaviour). If the decision of the said committee of judges recommends the removal of the Judge, it shall be a convention that the judge promptly demits office himself. If he fails to do so, the matter will be processed for being placed before Parliament in accordance with articles 124(4) and 217(1) Proviso (b). This procedure shall equally apply in case of Judges of the Supreme Court and the High Courts except that in the case of a Supreme Court Judge. The judge against whom complaint is received or inquiry is ordered shall not participate in any proceeding affecting him.

In appropriate cases the Chief Justice of the High Court or the Chief Justice of India, may withhold judicial work from the judge concerned after the inquiry committee records a finding against the judge.[64]

(3) Article 124(3) contemplates appointment of Judges of Supreme Court from three sources. However, in the last fifty years not a single distinguished jurist has been appointed. From the Bar also, less than half a dozen Judges have been appointed. It is time that suitably meritorious persons from these sources are appointed.[65]

(4) The retirement age of the Judges of the High Court should be increased to 65 years and that of the Judges of the Supreme Court should be increased to 68 years.[66]

(5) In the matter of transfer of Judges, it should be as a matter of policy and the power under article 222 and its exercise in appropriate cases should remain untouched. The President would transfer a Judge from one High Court to

any other High Court after consultation with a committee comprising the Chief Justice of India and the two senior-most Judges of the Supreme Court.[67]

(6) A proviso should be inserted in article 129 so as to provide that the power of court to punish for contempt of itself inherent only in the Supreme Court and the High Courts and is available as part of the privilege of Parliament and State Legislatures, and no other court, tribunal or authority should have or be conferred with a power to punish for contempt of itself.[68]

(7) A suitable provision may be inserted in the Constitution so as to provide that except the Supreme Court and the High Courts no other court, tribunal or authority shall exercise any jurisdiction to adjudicate on the validity or declare an Act of Parliament or State Legislature as being unconstitutional or beyond legislative competence and so *ultra vires*. Such a provision may be made as clause (5) of article 226.[69]

(8) 'Judicial Council' at the apex level and Judicial Councils at each State at the level of the High Court should be set-up. There should be an Administrative Office to assist the National Judicial Council and separate Administrative Offices attached to Judicial Councils in States. These bodies must be created under a statute made by Parliament. The Judicial Councils **should be in charge of** the preparation of plans, both short -term and long term, and for preparing the proposals for annual budget.[70]

(9) The budget proposals in each State must emanate from the State Judicial Council, in regard to the needs of the subordinate judiciary in that State, and will have to be submitted to the State Executive. Once the budget is so finalized between the State Judicial Council and the State Executive, it should be presented in the State Legislature.[71]

(10) The entire burden of establishing subordinate courts and maintaining subordinate judiciary should not be on the State Governments. There is a concurrent obligation on the Union Government to meet the expenditure for subordinate courts. Therefore, the Planning Commission and the Finance Commission must allocate sufficient

funds from national resources to meet the demands of the State judiciary in each of the States. [72]

(11) The presiding officers in courts should be adequately trained. To ensure competence, there should be a proper selection, freedom of action, training, motivation and experience. To maintain their competence, it is necessary to have continuing education for the judges. Some national judicial institutions have to be properly structured to give such training. There should be a proper monitoring of moving the judges where work demands such movement from places where there are no arrears of work. There has to be systematic assessment of training needs of judicial personnel at different levels.[73]

(12) The Government should ensure basic infrastructure needed to all courts and arrange to ensure that courts are not handicapped for want of infrastructural facilities. Governments, both at the Centre and in the States, should constitute committee of secretaries to review government litigation with a view to avoid adjudication, wherever possible, give priority in filling of written statements, wherever required, and instruct government advocates to seek early decision on government litigation.[74]

(13) In the Supreme Court and the High Courts, judgments should ordinarily be delivered not later than ninety days from the conclusion of the case. If a judgment is not rendered within such time - it is possible that the complexities of the case and the effect of the decision may have on another similar situation might compel greater and larger judicial consideration and contemplation - the case must be listed before the court immediately on the expiry of ninety days for the court to fix a specific date for the pronouncement of the judgment.[75]

(14) An award of exemplary costs should be given in appropriate cases for abuse of process of law.[76]

(15) The recommendations of the Law Commission of India in regard to the Nagar Nyayalayas, Conciliation Courts, ADR systems of urban litigation, evidence recording by Commissioners, etc. as incorporated in the Code of Civil Procedure (Amendment) Act, 2000 should be brought

into force with such modifications as it would take care of a few serious objections.[77]

(16) The provisions relating to conciliation in the Arbitration and Conciliation Act, 1996 should be suitably amended to provide for obligatory recourse to conciliation or mediation in relation to cases pending in courts. Further, the scope and functions of the Legal Services Authorities constituted under the Legal Services Authorities Act, 1987 should be enlarged and extended to enable the Authorities to set-up conciliation and mediation for and to conduct, in collaboration with other institutions wherever necessary, training courses for conciliators and mediators.[78]

(17) Each High Court should, in consultation with the judicial councils referred to in recommendation No. 129, prepare a strategic plan for time-bound clearance of arrears in courts under its jurisdiction. The plan may prescribe annual targets and district-wise performance targets. High Courts should establish monitoring mechanisms for progress evaluation. The purpose is to achieve the position that no court within the High Court's jurisdiction has any case pending for more than one year. This should be achieved within a period of five years or earlier.[79]

(18) The criminal investigation system needs higher standards of professionalised action and it should be provided with adequate logistic and technological support. Serious offences should be classified for purpose of specialized investigation by specially selected, trained and experienced investigators. They should not be burdened with other duties like security, maintenance of law and order etc., and should be entrusted exclusively with investigation of serious offences.[80]

(19) The number of Forensic Science Institutions with modern technologies such as DNA fingerprinting technology should be enhanced.[81]

(20) The system of Plea-Bargaining (as recommended by the Law Commission of India in its Report) should be introduced as part of the process of decriminalisation.[82]

(21) In order that citizen's confidence in the police administration is enhanced, the police administration in

the districts should periodically review the statistics of all the arrests made by the police in the district as to how many of the cases in which arrests were made culminated in the filing of charge-sheets in the court and how many of the arrests ultimately turned out to be unnecessary. This review will check the tendency of unnecessary arrests.[83]

(22) The Legal Services authorities in the States should set-up committees with the participation of civil society for bringing the accused and the victims together to work out compounding of offences.[84]

(23) Statements of witnesses during investigation of serious cases should be recorded before a magistrate under Section 164 of the Code of Criminal Procedure, 1973.[85]

(24) The case for a viable, social justice-oriented and effective scheme for compensation victims is now widely felt. The Government at the Union level and in the States are well advised under the directive principles as well as under International Human Rights obligations to legislate on the subject of an effective scheme of compensation for victims of crime without further delay.[86]

(25) The tremendous support which the criminal justice might derive from the people once the compensation scheme is introduced even in a modest scale, and the possibilities of advancing the crying need for social justice in a very real sense, are attractive enough for the State to find money to float the scheme immediately.[87]

(26) The National Informatics Centre in collaboration with or with the assistance of the Indian Law Institute and the Government Law Departments should set-up a Digital Legal Information System in the country so that all Courts, Legal Departments, Law schools would be able to access and retrieve information from the data bank of the important Law libraries in the country.[88]

(27) Progressively the hierarchy of the subordinate courts in the country should be brought down to a two-tier of subordinate judiciary under the High Court. Further, strict selection criteria and adequate training facilities for the presiding officers of such courts should be provided. In order to cope up with the workload of cases at the lower level and also to curtail arrears and delay, the States should

appoint Honorary Judicial Magistrates selected from experienced lawyers on the criminal side to try and dispose less serious and petty cases on part-time basis on the pattern of Recorders and Assistant Recorders in UK. They could set for, say, 100 days in a year and hold court later in the evenings after regular court hours. This would relieve the load on the regular magistracy.[89]

(28) Since the issues relating to human rights, more particularly relating to unlawful detention, have now occupied the centre-stage, both nationally and internationally, it shall be desirable that the Protection of Human Rights Act, 1993 may be suitably amended to provide that, in addition to the powers generally vested in that Court, such courts shall have the power to issue directions of the nature of a *habeas corpus* as was available to the High Courts under section 491 of the Code of Criminal Procedure, 1898. Vesting of such power will go a long way in providing help to the indigent and vulnerable sections of the society in view of the proximity and easy accessibility of the Court of Session.[90]

(c) Malimath Committee

Justice Malimath Committee under Chairmanship of Justice V.S. Malimath, former Chief Justice of Karnataka/Kerala High Court, was constituted by Govt. of India to revamp Criminal Justice System. The Committee submitted its report to the Government of India on March 2003. The terms of reference of the Committee were:

(i) To examine the fundamental principle of criminal jurisprudence, including the constitutional provisions relating to criminal jurisprudence and see if any modifications or amendments are required thereto.

(ii) To examine in the light of findings on fundamental principles and aspects of criminal jurisprudence as to whether there is a need to rewrite the Code of Criminal Procedure, the Indian Penal Code and the Indian Evidence Act to bring them in tune with the demand of the times and in harmony with the aspirations of the people of India.

(iii) To make specific recommendations on simplifying judicial procedures and practices and making the delivery of justice to the common man closer, faster, uncomplicated and inexpensive.

(iv) To suggest ways and means of developing such synergy among the Judiciary, the prosecution and the police restores the confidence of the common man in the criminal justice system by protecting the innocent and the victim by punishing unsparingly the guilty and the criminal.

(v) To suggest sound system of managing on professional lines, the pendency of cases at investigation and trial stages making the police, the prosecution and the judiciary accountable for delays in their respective domains.

(vi) To examine the feasibility of introducing the concept of federal crime which can be put on List-I in the Seventh Schedule to the Constitution of India

In its report the Committee has observed that there is huge backlog of criminal cases in the country and unless concerted efforts are made on a war-footing, the position will not improve and people will continue to suffer. On the basis of terms of reference the Malimath Committee made the following recommendations:[91]

1. Abolition of Original Civil Jurisdiction of the High Court.
2. Abolition of Letters Patent Appeals.
3. Filing of certified copy of decree to be dispensed with.
4. High Courts to specify categories of cases which could be heard by Single Judge, or by a Division Bench.
5. Magisterial Courts to try in a summary way the offences specified in Sections 260 and 261 of the Criminal Procedure Code.
6. Work of serving summons and notices should be entrusted to the process servers of the courts in addition to the police at present.
7. Convention to be evolved that would discourage granting adjournments.
8. Court should avoid writing long and elaborate judgments.
9. Reserved judgments should ordinarily be delivered within a reasonable time.
10. Court to prepare lists of old cases and arrange their early disposal.

The Malimath Committee made another set of recommendations for setting up of Alternative Tribunals to reduce pendency in High Courts besides the following:

1. Setting up of Industrial Relations Commission.
2. Setting up of Rent Tribunals.
3. Extension of Jurisdiction of Central Administrative Tribunals to the teaching and non-teaching staff of universities. Earlier teaching and non-teaching staffs were not covered by the CAT's jurisdiction.
4. Setting up of tribunal/machinery for early disposal of cases concerning students' admissions/examination malpractices, educational programmes, affiliation and de-affiliation of colleges, election to universities/bodies, etc.[92]

Setting up of alternative tribunals viz. Industrial Relations Commissions; Rent Tribunals; and setting up of tribunals with jurisdiction on various educational malpractices are likely to help reduce the burden on courts.

Alternative Mode of Dispute Settlement

Considering the mammoth size of arrears, alternative modes of dispute settlement are the best way to reduce the number of cases filed everyday. The Malimath Committee and Chief Ministers and Chief Justices Conference, 1993 made recommendations on this aspect and a Bill to amend Civil Procedure Code i.e. The Code, of Civil Procedure (Amendment) Bill, 1997 was brought which contained *inter alia* provisions for making it obligatory for the court to refer the dispute after the issues are framed for settlement either by way of arbitration conciliation, mediation, judicial settlement or through Lok Adalat. It is only after parties fail to get their disputes settled through alternative dispute resolution methods that the suit shall proceed further in the court in which it was failed.[93]

It is expected that efforts of this kind would definitely help reduce the burden on the courts and decrease the accumulation of arrears. The Committee feels that the government should encourage Non-government organizations to spread awareness among the people especially people of low-income groups, about the futility of frivolous cases to be filed in the court and persuade them to adopt methods like arbitration, mediation, and other modes of out of the court settlement. The Committee is of the view that an enlightened Bar and the Bar Councils have a crucial role to play in the process.

4. INITIATIVES TAKEN BY THE SUPREME COURT

The Supreme Court has taken certain steps which have resulted in a substantial reduction in accumulated arrears. It has successfully implemented the cardinal principles of Active Case-flow Management Technique (ACMT) by creating dual tracks, one for keeping abreast of current filings and the other to deal with old pending matters. It is a model which commends itself to us and which can be replicated for dealing with the arrears in the High Courts and Subordinate Courts. A report on "**Modernization of Civil Justice System in India: Implementation Plan**", prepared by the Study Team Constituted by the National Judicial Academy and submitted to the Hon'ble Chief Justice of India, may be referred to for detailed discussion on the monitoring, co-ordination and case-flow tracking.

Another area where the Apex Court has concentrated its energy is on adjournments. Adjournments have been made an exception. Now adjournments in Supreme Court can never be taken for granted and cases scheduled for a particular date are invariably listed on that day. Indeed, listing is entirely computer managed, except for extremely urgent listing required within less than 15 days for which a special oral mention has to be made to the Chief Justice.

In the Apex Court, the cases listed for a day which were earlier adjourned owing to the absence of any Judge are now immediately redistributed on the very day over the remaining Benches and thus dealt with or disposed of on the same day, despite an inevitably enhanced work load for each bench.

Bench stabilization in the Apex Court over three-month or six-month periods ensures that the same or similar subjects out of the 56 computer classified subjects go to the same Benches as far as possible, thus expediting disposal.

On the Human Resource Front, the Apex Court has made efforts to streamline the distribution of work in all the departments in such a way that intra-departmental and inter-departmental file movement can be minimized. It has reorganized the staff strength depending on the filings and pendency.

The Apex Court has made use of the computer in the most effective way. Computerization at every level in the Department of Registry has increased efficiency considerably. Maximum information covering numerous fields and criteria are fed into the computer in respect of each case, thus ensuring maximum information retrieval at the touch of a button and a Judis Programme has already incorporated all the Supreme Court judgments into the computer.

In addition, the following steps have also been taken in the Apex Court:

a) More practical categorization and grouping of cases involving similar questions of law.
b) No accumulation of defective matters; and
c) Reservation of sufficient slots for old, pending, miscellaneous and Special Leave Petition matters so that they are listed in Chronological order in sufficient numbers.

It is significant that despite poor infrastructure and other constraints in lower courts they have made a dent, howsoever small, on the problem of arrears. Those courts deserve better facilities and better working conditions. All necessary steps may be taken to secure expeditious handling of cases in the High Courts and the Subordinate Courts by filling the vacancies of Judges; application of Active Case-flow Management Technique (ACMT); stricter control over adjournments; reallocation of cases when a bench is unable to sit; bench stabilization; and manpower management to reduce time taken in file movement. Need is felt for giving top priority to improve manpower and infrastructural facilities at the Subordinate/District Court levels so as to facilitate wiping out of the arrears and swift disposal of cases. Budgetary allocations have to be augmented substantially. There is need for a greater sense of purpose.

In a step towards creating a speedy justice delivery system, 2014 will see the Supreme Court of India working more than in 2013. In a bid to lessen the pendency of cases that has already crossed the mark of three crores, Chief Justice of India P. Sathasivam has cut down the number of holidays of the Supreme Court from 2014 onwards.

As per the Supreme Court's calendar for 2014, of the 365 days, the court will work for nearly 200 days whereas in 2013, the court worked for nearly 176 days and 189 days were holidays which included roughly 104 Saturdays and Sundays, and nearly two-and-a-half months of summer vacations.

The British legacy of a nearly two-month-long summer vacation is still a continuing tradition in the apex court. As per the provisions of the Supreme Court Judges (Salaries and Conditions of Service) Act, 1958, besides the apex court's holidays and vacations, the individual judges are also entitled to their own quota of leave.

Depending on the number of years a judge puts in the service, he is entitled to certain days of leave on full salary, certain other offs on half salary and some more days off on one quarter salary.

Data from the Department of Justice reveals that the total number of cases pending in the apex court has gone up from last year and has already crossed 65,000 this year.

In 2009, the Law Commission in its 230th report had stated that vacations in the higher judiciary should be curtailed by at least 10 to 15 days and the court working hours should be extended by at least half an hour.

"Considering the huge pendency of cases at all levels of judicial hierarchy, it has become necessary to increase the number of working days. It has to be introduced at all levels of judicial hierarchy and must start from the apex court.

With the increase in the salaries and perks of the Judges, it is their moral duty to respond commensurately," the commission report had then stated.

The Law Commission's report, which is under consideration of Chief Justice of India and all the respective Chief Justices of High Courts, also highlighted the need of ensuring speedy justice. It noted, "Speedy justice is the right of every litigating person. There is no denying the fact that delay frustrates justice. In the present set-up it often takes 10, 20, 30 or even more years before a matter is finally decided."[94]

Reports of the Law Commission of India

Law Commission of India delved into the problem of delay in trial of criminal cases and suggested many remedial measures from time to time. To protect the human rights of the accused by speedy trial, the following important recommendations have been made by the Law Commission and National Police Commission in its reports from time to time:

a) To separate the investigating wing from the wing entrusted with the enforcement of law and order in the Police Department.[95]

b) To provide sufficient funds to the Judiciary to increase the existing number of criminal courts, with sufficient supporting staff including stenographers and to modernize the subordinate judiciary with equipment like xerox machines, electronic typewriters and computers.[96]

c) To make statutory provision for settlement of disputes by conciliatory Board under the supervision of subordinate criminal court.[97]

d) To depute one Senior Additional District and Sessions Judge in each district for devoting whole time in monitoring disposal of old cases by making monthly inspection of each court and co-ordination with other functionaries of the district, government and High Court.[98]

e) To recruit young talented law graduates in Judiciary by creating Indian Judicial Service.[99]

f) To train Judicial Officers by establishing National Academy for Training of Judicial Officers.[100]

g) To establish a prosecuting agency with all infrastructures, so that it may work not only as a legal wing of the police department but also as an effective segment of Criminal Justice System.[101]

h) To institute Gram Nyayalayas to deal with ordinary crimes and disposal of petty cases at taluk level.[102]

5. LAW COMMISSION OF INDIA REPORT 2012 ON EXPEDITIOUS INVESTIGATION AND TRIAL OF CRIMINAL CASES AGAINST INFLUENTIAL PUBLIC PERSONALITIES[103]

Then arises the question as to whether and to what extent directions should be given within the framework of existing laws to ensure that public men do not, by virtue of their influence and power, interfere with the process of investigation and do not create impediments in the way of expeditious and continuous trial. Though there could be special focus on the criminal cases involving influential public men, the steps to be taken should be part of the larger plan to check delays and deficiencies in investigation into serious crimes and to ensure progress of trials without hindrances and hurdles placed by the accused. There must be holistic approach. By and large, the measures contemplated should equally apply to other criminal cases involving serious crimes, irrespective of who the accused is. There must be special focus on old cases including those relating to public men and the bottlenecks in the way of progress should be removed. The suggestions are formulated in this Report, accordingly.

1. Some measures that may be directed to be taken by the Police after FIR is received/recorded

(i) A copy of FIR concerning the involvement of influential public men in cognizable crimes, apart from being sent to the Magistrate, should also be forwarded to SP/SSP concerned.

(ii) The investigation should be taken up promptly and with expedition [unless the police officer concerned forms an opinion under clause (b) of the proviso to Section 157(1) Cr.P.C]. The SP/SSP shall, from time to time, get reports from the SHO regarding the course and progress of investigation and issue suitable instructions. He may render such assistance as may be required by the SHO in this regard, to wit, providing additional police force, securing reports from the forensic science laboratories expeditiously etc.

(iii) The investigation shall be completed as far as possible within three months and at any rate not later than six months. The charge-sheet shall be filed within a month thereafter along with requisite documents properly indexed. A copy of the draft charge-sheet to be sent to SP/SSP for vetting.

(iv) The FIR, the statement of accused and witnesses examined and the record prepared by I.O. from time to time should be computerized so that they could be made available to all concerned in an electronic form (non-re-recordable compact disc).

(v) The I.O., SP/SSP should be held personally responsible for the failure to ensure that the investigation is completed within the specified time limit and they shall face disciplinary proceedings for non-compliance, unless they establish that reasonably diligent steps were being taken by them. The responsibility lies with the DGP to initiate such disciplinary action as may be warranted.

(vi) The SP/SSP should maintain a record of FIRs in respect of influential public persons so as to enable him to keep track of such cases from time to time.

(vii) In cases involving influential public personalities, resort to S. 164 Cr.P.C. should be made more frequently.

(viii) While investigation of offences under the provisions of Cr. P.C. is the exclusive domain of the police, the Judl. Magistrate should have limited role to play to counter the moves of persons in influential positions to subvert the effective process of investigation. Accordingly, the I.O. shall bring to the notice of Magistrate the bottlenecks, if any, that are coming in the way of speedy investigation including the attempts being made by the accused to hinder the investigation. The Magistrate shall, apart from taking such steps as are permissible under law, for example, issuing summons for the production of documents in the custody of suspect/accused a third party, may also send up a report to the District Judge for appropriate action on the administrative side to eliminate delays.

(ix) In respect of serious crimes i.e. cognizable and punishable with imprisonment of 5 years or more irrespective of whether public men are involved, if investigation has not been completed within 6 months, a report has to be submitted by the I.O. to the SP/SSP who shall take necessary action to ensure completion of investigation. The SPs/SSPs should maintain a register of such cases where there are delays in investigation and should take remedial steps to remove the bottlenecks.

(x) The photograph of the accused and full address/phone numbers, e-mail I.D. if any, shall be obtained and the photos be affixed to the arrest Memo and Charge-sheet. (This is being done in some States e.g. Maharashtra).

(xi) The Police should take requisite steps to ensure proper and prompt maintenance of medico-legal registers maintained at the hospitals.

1.1 Duty of Police in cases where there are no formal complaints : Whenever credible information is received by the Police (SHO) that a cognizable crime is committed by a public servant or an important public personality, it is his duty to register the crime. For instance, the corruption may be exposed by sting operations which are aired in TV or published in media. They should act on them, subject to verification of the authenticity of report. Anirudha Bahal's case[104] decided by Delhi High Court brings to light the lapse of police in this regard.

1.2 In this context, it is pointed out that the provisions contained in Sections 154 and 157 read with Section 156 confer sufficient powers on the Police officer to initiate investigation.

1.3 Whenever statutory sanctions are required for prosecution of public servants and others, the Government concerned should act with expedition. Normally, it should be done within 3 or 4 months.[105] The Secretary in charge of the Department should ensure this.

2. Measures to be taken after the Court is seized off the matter (during trial)

a) The cases in which delays are occurring in cognizable cases against influential public persons as well as others by reason of conduct of the accused or inaction on the part of the Police or prosecution, should be brought to the notice of District Judge who shall, if necessary, take up the issue with the SP/SSP.

b) In Sessions cases, if there are inordinate delays attributable to the accused/Police/prosecution, and the ADJs trying the case feel helpless, it should be brought to the notice of District Judge who shall apprise the SP/SSP of the problem at the earliest and alert them to initiate necessary action by way of apprehending the accused or producing the witnesses. Inspite of that if the Police do not respond, the District Judge shall send up a special report to the High Court **especially** if the case relates to an influential public person.

c) Similarly, the District Judge should inform the High Court wherever inordinate delays are experienced by the District Judge in the trial of Sessions cases and the SP/SSP is not taking sufficient action.

d) There must be special drive to secure the attendance of Proclaimed offenders.

e) Applications for witness protection should be promptly disposed off by the trial Courts by giving appropriate directions to the Police.

f) There must be a Special Cell in the High Court exclusively to take stock of old pending Sessions cases. The cell headed by a Registrar level officer should promptly bring to the notice of the concerned Administrative/Portfolio Judge or any other Judge/Committee nominated by the Chief Justice for this purpose, the factum of pendency of such cases, the District Judge's report, if any, and the reasons furnished for prolongation of the cases. It is desirable that the Judges of High Court who have comparatively less administrative work, are entrusted with the job of taking effective measures to check the delays and pave the way for early conclusion of criminal trials. In this process, the concerned Administrative/Portfolio Judge may also be associated. The Special Cell should regularly coordinate with the Committee. The said Committee based on the information received from the District Judge in the quarterly statement or otherwise, should take necessary measures on the administrative side to remove the bottlenecks in the progress of trial, for instance, by way of giving necessary instructions to the DGP/DIG/SP.

g) In the quarterly statements also, the District Judges should record brief reasons for the delay in Sessions cases which are more than 3 years old from the date of framing the charges and *inter-alia* they must state **whether the case relates to an influential public person.**

h) Top priority should be given to the Sessions cases especially those related to influential public persons which are more than 5 years old (or even less depending on the workload position). The concerned High Court Committee should bestow special attention to such cases and review the progress from time to time so that the trial concludes most expeditiously. If necessary, the Committee may take steps for the transfer of such cases to the Court having less workload. Obviously, however, the Committee of High Court ought not to say anything even indirectly on the merits of the case, even if obstructionist tactics are adopted by the accused for some reason or the other.

i) The norm of continuity of trial shall be strictly observed in all cases (above 5 year old or even less depending on the workload position), more especially in the cases related to important political persons. As a part of case management process, a calendar of dates should be drawn up for trial in consultation with the learned advocates and PP and the timeschedule shall be substantially adhered to. The High Court may, from time to time issue circulars stressing the need to adhere to the timeschedule and refusal of adjournments (unless there are special and exceptional reasons) and they shall be exhibited on the notice-board of the Court and Bar Association. By assuming a more proactive role in taking various measures as stated above, the High Courts will only be acting within the purview of the jurisdiction and authority conferred on them under Articles 235 and 227 of the Constitution of India as well as Section 483 of Cr.P.C. However, to make the position more clear, certain amendments to Cr.P.C. as per Annexure are desirable. High Courts have to frame Rules or issue Circulars in exercise of the powers conferred by the proposed provisions in Annexure. In any case, the High Courts can very well invoke Art. 235 of the Constitution to play their due role in ensuring speedy disposal of criminal cases.

j) The High Court, on the judicial side, should give top priority to the disposal of quash petitions/revisions in the pending trial matters. Records are not to be called for in such cases unless the perusal of any original document is found necessary. The trial can go on unless there is specific order of stay and this can be made clear by a circular issued by High Court.

k) The Special Cell should bring to the notice of Chief Justice from time to time the Sessions and other cases involving major crimes pending trial in which proceedings are stayed or the records are called for. In this connection, the recent judgment of Supreme Court in *Imtiyaz Ahmed* v. *State of U.P.*[106] is quite relevant.

l) Any representation by the aggrieved persons or victims regarding undue delay in the disposal of criminal cases shall receive due attention of the District Judge as well as the High Court Committee. Any such representations received by the Registry should be forwarded to the Special Cell.

m) The Special Cell should also keep record of Sessions Cases or other cases punishable with imprisonment of more than 3 years against the advocates, as pointed out by the Law Commission of India in its written submissions to the Allahabad High Court (Lucknow Bench) in W.P. No. 9925 (M/B) of 2010, and place the information before the Committee of Judges so that appropriate directions may be given by the Committee to ensure early disposal of such cases.

3. Need for ear-marked Police Personnel for Court duties

3.1 The most conspicuous reason for the delays in the progress of trial is non-execution of warrants by the Police. Unserved summons and non-bailable warrants (NBWs) have a telling effect on the Criminal Justice scenario. Police inaction, indifference or inability are the contributory factor to the grim situation of pendency of large number of unexecuted NBWs. The cases get adjourned from time to time because of non-appearance of one or some of the accused. Police plead their inability to apprehend the accused (against whom NBWs and Proclamation orders have been issued) for good and bad reasons. The fact remains that Police do not consider it as a priority item and they act in a casual and routine manner. Even the prominent accused (holding a public position or leading a political party) are shown as absconding or not available for contact, as demonstrated by the case on hand. There is only one Police Constable attached to each Criminal Court and some times that single Constable attends to the work of two courts. He acts as a post office to carry the summons/warrants to the Police Station and leave it to the SHO to act on it. There are innumerable instances in which the Police Officer concerned does not even send up a report to the Court as to the stage of NBW and the specific reason for non-apprehension of the accused. In the State of Jharkhand, the feedback is that warrants remain unexecuted for months and years as the

Police personnel are not available for attending to this work, in as much as they are deployed on duty in remote and sensitive areas to cope up with the extremist menace, etc.

3.2 In almost all the States, periodical meetings of District Judge with SSP/SP take place and in such meetings, the pendency of unexecuted NBWs and the progress made since the last meetings, are reviewed. So also, when the Administrative/Portfolio Judges go on visits to the concerned districts, the Supdts. of Police are instructed to expedite the execution of warrants. Such meetings convened by the District Judge and the instructions of the High Court Judge during his/her occasional visits do yield some results. Still, the problem substantially remains. The responses of the Police Officers are, by and large, *ad hoc*. Whenever there is pressure from the side of the judiciary, a special squad will be set-up to apprehend the accused, but the tempo subsides after some time. In the State of U.P., it appears that there is a Summons Cell of Police in every district which is assigned the work of executing the summons/warrants. But, either the force attached to that cell is inadequate or their services are diverted quite often to other jobs. Needless to state that the execution of warrants needs constant attention and surveillance. The Police plead genuine difficulties to devote the required attention for this item of work. It is a well known fact that Police Stations are understaffed and ill-equipped.

Having regard to these problems and keeping in view the inputs received from the District Judges and other Judicial Officers of various States, the Law Commission is of the view that dedicated Police personnel should be put in place to attend exclusively to Court-related duties viz., service of summons and execution of warrants. The number of personnel required for each Court may be in the range of 2 to 4. Such Police personnel should work under the supervision of an Inspector of Police (exclusively deployed for this purpose) and the Inspector should report to the District Judge every month. They must be imparted training for atleast 4 weeks and should be provided with necessary infrastructure. SP level officer should monitor the work of this Police force attending to court-related duties. Such senior Police officer should be nominated for a region or a group of districts. Posting of such senior Police officer shall be in consultation with the Registrar-General of High Court. Alternatively, each Police station should have sufficient number of Head Constables and Constables exclusively deployed for Court-related duties. They should have sufficient infrastructure such as additional accommodation with a lock-up cell. The SHO should send monthly or bi-monthly reports to the concerned courts stating details of progress made.

3.3 There was a suggestion from some quarters that armed reserve Police who do not have much of work may be drafted for these duties till a regular cadre is constituted. This can be examined. However, the regular Police shall not shed their responsibility of extending necessary cooperation to the special Police personnel.

3.4 Before giving any direction in this regard, it is perhaps necessary that the State Governments shall be put on notice and their views, if any, are ascertained. Thereafter, the DGPs should be directed to initiate action in this behalf without delay.

3.5 There is one more aspect related to the same problem which needs to be tackled particularly. There are consistent reports that the execution of warrants against the accused, residing or staying in other States, has become a formidable problem. For years together, the warrants remain unexecuted and the out-of-state accused remain absent. The requisitions sent by the CJM or the Sessions Judge to the Police Officer and/or the CJMs of other States evoke no response from the police and Judicial officers of other States. In a few cases, the Police personnel of the State in which the case is pending, are sent to the other State to trace and arrest the accused. Even then, they can effect the arrest of the wanted person only with the cooperation of the Police of the other State. Quite often, even that cooperation will not be forthcoming. The Law Commission is of the view that the concerned SSP/SP of the other State should be made responsible for complying with the requisition sent by the Court in which the case is pending and it shall be made mandatory to send reports on the steps being taken by the Police at least once in a month to the Court which has issued the warrant. The communication should be sent electronically or by fax. The court concerned shall be required to furnish the fax and e-mail particulars. The District Judges of other States during their conferences with senior Police officers, should review the steps taken to execute NBWs issued by the Courts of Magistrates/Sessions Judges of the State in which the case is being dealt with. The District Judges should maintain a record of such requisitions received on the basis of the information furnished by CJMs/Magistrates.

4. Strengthening Prosecution Machinery

As already pointed out, the prosecution machinery is in shambles. There is need to empower the Directorate of Prosecution with independent powers for effectively supervising the working off PPs/APPs. The recruitment/appointment process should be transparent and objective based on merit and experience. Their conditions of service needs to be improved considerably. There must be intensive training and refresher courses and periodical review meetings. It is of utmost importance that vacancies of PPs/APPs are filled up promptly. There is every need to create additional posts as well.

5. Increase in the number of courts and filling up of vacancies promptly

5.1 In All India Judges Association case[107] the Supreme Court, on a comparative assessment of the position existing in other countries, directed that there should be 50 judges for a million population as recommended by the Parliamentary Standing Committee (Rajya Sabha) 85th report[108] as well as recommended by the Law Commission of India in its 120th Report.[109] The Court noticed that the sanctioned strength of judges then existing was only 10.5 (or 13) per one million. Though the Supreme Court directed that there should be addition of courts in a phased manner, very little progress has been made. Many State Governments plead financial difficulties for the creation of so many courts. The proportion which the present sanctioned strength of judges bears to the total population is about 15 per one million. The docket ratio per Judge in the District and Subordinate Judiciary is approximately 1630 cases. This is based on sanctioned strength. The unfortunate part of it is that at any given point of time, about 20% of the vacancies of Judl. Officers remain unfilled. This is on account of lack of proper planning on the part of the High Courts, coupled with inordinate delays in recruitment process and promotions. Further, delayed promotions naturally give rise to considerable heartburn among the members of the service.

5.2 It may be stated that with the setting up of Fast Track Sessions Courts in most of the States, lot of pendency has been cleared, as far as the Sessions cases are concerned. The Central Government has stopped funding such courts from April 2011. However, in many States, FT Sessions courts are continuing with

State funding up to March 2012. While much progress has been achieved in the disposal of sessions cases, the pendency has increased in Magistrates courts. This is by reason of quicker promotions earned by Jr. Civil Magistrates as a result of setting up of Fast Track Sessions Courts and the resultant vacancies in that cadre adding to the existing vacancies. The pendency in some of the courts of First Class Judicial Magistrates and Chief Judicial Magistrates runs into thousands and it is at an unmanageable level. Keeping this in view, the 13th Finance Commission has evolved a scheme for setting up of a large number of Fast Track Special Magistrates Courts (Evening Courts/Shift Courts) to deal with the cases involving minor offences and simpler matters. Summary trial cases, cases under section 125 Cr. P.C., cases under section 138 of NI Act, traffic offences (other than those under MV Act) are to be assigned to these Magistrates. The Central Government meets the expenditure initially. There is a huge financial provision made for Gram Nyayalayas also. Certain practical difficulties are being experienced in making these courts operational. The dearth of judicial officers and staff is being felt and in some States like UP, it is reported that the lawyers are not in favour of Evening/Morning Courts.

5.3 There is an allied problem of inadequate staff strength in the Courts, inefficient staff and large number of vacancies of essential posts like stenographers and staff having knowledge of computer operation. Further, the data posted on the website is not updated promptly. The lack of proper servicing facilities in the District and moffusil areas is resulting in the computers remaining in disrepair, un-rectified for months together. Moreover, the recruitment process followed by the courts needs to be refined so as to facilitate induction of efficient and competent candidates.

6. Other Issues

6.1 The issues relating to setting up of new courts and filling up of vacancies is engaging the attention of this Hon'ble Court before a Bench presided over by Hon'ble Justice D.K. Jain in two matters *Janhit Manch* v. *UOI*[110] and *Malik Mazhar Sultan* v. *Union Public Service Commission*[111]. The subject related to infrastructure for the Courts is being monitored by another Bench headed by Hon'ble Chief Justice of India in W.P. No. 1022 of 1989. Further, in a recent judgment (*Imtiyaz Ahmed* v. *State of U.P.*)[112] of this Hon'ble Court, the Law Commission of India has been entrusted with the task of ascertaining the number of additional Courts needed in the country after consulting the concerned Stakeholders. In view of this, there is perhaps no need for this Hon'ble Bench to go into the issue relating to inadequate number of courts and infrastructure in depth.

6.2 The need for dedicated police personnel attached to the criminal courts for service of summons and warrants has been dealt with in paragraph 9.1, page 26 above. It is necessary that having regard to the magnitude of the problem and the imminent need to speed up criminal justice, this Hon'ble Court be pleased to give appropriate directions to the State Governments and Governments of Union Territories in this regard.

6.3 Separation of investigation from law and order duties: Directions given in *Prakash Singh's case*[113] have not so far complied with except in a few Police Stations. The Commission does not propose to discuss this aspect firstly, for the reason that there is already a direction of the Supreme Court, secondly, there is already the report of Law Commission (154th report) recommending such separation, and thirdly, it involves interaction with both senior and junior level Police officials, which is a time consuming process.

7. Other important measures to improve Crl. Justice

7.1 It is submitted that two important steps are ideally required for speeding up the criminal justice in the hope that this will also augment the conviction rate. These are as under:

(a) Deployment of technology at the level of Police stations.

(b) Strengthening Criminal Courts' infrastructure and upgrading facilities and amenities therein. These steps have to be taken up in a phased manner after due planning.

The detailed suggestions under the above two heads are as under:

A. *Deployment of Technology at the Police Stations*

a) *Recording of FIRs*

It is found that many of the acquittals are due to the delay, ante timing and absence of the necessary details of the incident in the FIRs. This one single factor can be eliminated by providing for compulsory and automatic recording of all landlines provided in the Police Stations. There should also be a provision for automatic relay of the telephone conversation between the caller and Police Station operator to all the Patrol vehicles of the Police deployed in the area to reduce the response time of Police. The patrol vehicles should also have connectivity with the Police net for knowing the antecedents of the suspects/vehicles/documents etc. on the spot and instantly. FIRs shall be recorded on the computer and they shall be instantly sent to the Magistrates' Courts by e-mail. The practice of sending FIR through e-mail should be legally recognized. Similarly, section 161 statements should also be placed on the computer and posted on the website of the concerned court.

b) *Police Stations: Modernization*

(i) Networking of all police stations to establish a link with all the courts.

(ii) Digital videography to be installed at police stations. At the time of receiving FIR/complaint, videography should be made compulsory. By this process, the earliest version of the informant will be evident. So also, at the time of inspection of the scene of offence and recovery of material objects, videography should be insisted upon.

(iii) Interrogation Rooms: Each Police Station should be provided with secure interrogation rooms, with simultaneous audio-visual recording facilities by two cameras, one focusing on the close-up of the face of the witness or the suspect and the second giving a wide angled picture to show that there is no coercion to influence the statement of the witness or the suspect. Statement of all suspects and witnesses should, by law, be required to be recorded in such windowless interrogation rooms with mirrors on the two walls. The question of treating as admissible, the statements of the accused and witnesses examined in secure interrogation rooms deserve serious consideration.

c) *Mobile Forensic Vans*

At least, all District Headquarters should be provided with mobile forensic vans which should accompany the homicide teams to the place of occurrence. The mobile forensic vans should be equipped with equipment for instant blood test and finger print comparison, on the spot, in addition to the facilities of lifting the finger prints and blood samples from the scene of crime. The vans should also have provision for video-recording of the scene of crime as well as that of searches and seizures on the spot. In the Districts where NDPS crimes are more, narcotics testing kits should be provided to every Police Station.

d) Charge-sheets by CDs

All charge-sheets should be required to be submitted in electronic form on a non-re-writable compact disc wherever such facility exists. A suitable amendment to S. 173 can be thought of for this purpose. Police can be required to submit as many CDs as the number of accused figuring in the charge sheets. This will reduce considerable delays that take place in the cases triable by Court of Sessions.

B. Strengthening criminal courts' infrastructure and upgrading facilities therein

1. **Properly designed Court Complexes**: It is essential that a standardized design of the criminal court complex be prescribed by the High Court which shall *inter alia* take care of separate rooms for witnesses, undertrial prisoners, Police personnel, advocates and prosecutors and shall provide for sufficient number of washrooms and filtered drinking water facilities.

2. **Summons etc.—Service**: All court notices, summons for appearance or summons for production of documents may be served through e-mail and in the absence of the e-mail of the addressees, through the e-mail of the police station, which must report compliance with regard to the service on a weekly basis through e-mails.

As regards official witnesses, in order to avoid delays in service, the summons can be sent through email or if the email ID is not ascertainable, the summons can be sent to the Head of Office (for instance, District Medical Officer who has administrative control over the hospitals.) All bail orders to be communicated to the Jail through e-mail for delivery to the undertrial prisoners.

3. **Recording of evidence**: All criminal courts ought to be provided with Audio recording through tamper-proof technology for recording of statements of witnesses so that the appellate courts can also refer to the same for determining the exact statement made by the witnesses.

4. **Machines:** All criminal courts ought to be provided with transcription machines with the help of which the Audio-recorded statements can automatically be transcribed and supplied to the counsel and witnesses on the same day.

5. **Conferencing**: In order to interact with undertrial prisoners and police officials, video-conferencing facility needs to be provided. So also, videoconferencing will be very useful for the interaction between High Court and District Judges. It would save lot of time and resources and help in fulfilling the formalities without delay.

6. **Witness Rooms**: All criminal courts ought to be provided with a separate witness room where witnesses, who have been summoned in different courts, be provided with the facilities of comfortable seating, drinking water, urinals, tea/coffee machine and some reading material. It needs to be appreciated that witnesses are the eyes and ears of the court and the court needs them more for dispensing justice than they need the court. This will also enable them to be saved from the harassment they have to face at the hands of the accused as they also wait in the same corridors.

7. **Centralized Registry**: All criminal courts located in a single or nearby complex must have a centralized record room instead of separate record keeping for each court. The centralized record keeping will ensure that the relevant part of the file is placed before the concerned court as and when required.

8. **Stenographers**: Competent stenographers with good knowledge of computer operation and maintenance to be attracted to judicial service by offering higher pay and facilities.

Amendment to Section 477 Cr.P.C.

[e] providing for supervision and monitoring towards expeditious disposal of cases pending over a long period, or such categories or classes of cases having regard to their impact on administration of justice or public interest. [The rules may provide both for administrative and judicial supervision.]

Amendment to Section 483 Cr.P.C:

The existing provision may be substituted by the following:

[1] Every High Court shall so exercise its superintendence over

[a] all courts subordinate to it under this Code, and

[b] courts from whose orders or judgments appeals or revision lie to the High Court, so as to ensure expeditious and proper disposal of cases by such courts.

[2] The Public Prosecutor, the complainant or any other person on behalf of the victim/injured or deceased may apply to the High Court seeking exercise of the above-said power of superintendence.

A New Provision—Section 157A

Any time after the passing of an order under sub-section (2) of Section 155 relating to investigation of non-cognizable cases or after receipt of a report under sub-Section (1) of Section 156, relating to investigation of cognizable cases, the court concerned, either *suo motu* or on an application by the public prosecutor, or any other person acting on behalf of the deceased, injured or the victim of the offence, may call for information regarding the investigation of the case and issue such directions as may be necessary to facilitate expeditious investigation without in any way prejudicing the manner of investigation.

Chairman – (Justice P.V. Reddi)
Members – 1. Justice Shiv Kumar Sharma
2. Amarjit Singh
3. Dr Brahm Agrawal (Member-Secretary)

Initiative taken by the Government

To reduce delay and increase the rate of disposal of cases, the Government of India proposes to computerize all the lower courts in the country. A scheme for computerization of all the 13,000 District and Subordinate courts, prepared in accordance with the National Policy and Action Plan, has been approved by the Government of India on 8th February 2007 with National Informatics Centre (NIC) as the implementing Agency. The coverage of the project includes Information and Communication Technology (ICT) enablement of all the Districts and Subordinate Courts of the Country and upgrading the infrastructure of the Supreme Court and all the High Courts.[114]

The project is to be implemented in three phases over a period of five years. The first phase, which is under implementation, is scheduled to be completed by the end of the year 2009. The implementation of the project will go a long way in reducing the huge back-log of cases.

6. CONCLUSION

After going through the pros and cons of the chapter, it can be concluded that the alternative dispute resolution mechanisms are the best possible to resolve disputes between the parties. ADR mechanisms provide for more effective resolution of disputes as the parties are more involved in the process and the process is swift. Court processes that are traditionally practiced may not in every case provide the best approach towards the resolution of disputes. For instance, in the case of matrimonial disputes, which are sensitive in nature, involving both legal as well as emotional questions, the parties are not interested in winning or losing, but in reaching a solution. Inordinate delays that are a part of the ordinary legal process may emotionally affect the parties and cause frustration. The matter may be more effectively resolved, if it is not dealt within a mechanical and technical manner. The procedures employed in Alternate Dispute Resolution are flexible and informal in contrast to the formal and rigid procedures followed in the ordinary process of dispute resolution in courts of law. These processes thus facilitate access to justice. So it is high time that an immediate solution to the growing backlog of cases is sought on a priority basis so that the confidence of the people in the judicial system remains intact. If this is not done on a priority basis it would not only be the defeat of our constitutional philosophy but also contribute to the collapse of our entire judicial system.

Notes and References

1. Prof. Anurag K. Agarwal, "*Strenthening the Lok Adalat Movement in India*", AIR, March, 2006 (Journal Section); p. 33.
2. Articles 32-35, The Constitution of India.
3. M.K. Gandhi; '*The Law and the Lawyers*'; Navjivan Trust, Ahmedabad, 1962, Reprint 2001; p. 258.
4. *Supra* Note 1; at p. 33.
5. *Id.* at p. 34.
6. Figure was given by Chief Justice K.G. Balakrishnan while inaugurating the "All India Seminar on Judicial Reform" held 23rd-25th Feb. 2008.
7. *Supra* Note -5 at p. 35.
8. *Id.* at p. 37.

9. B.M. Manoj; "*Future of ADR in India,*" Published in *Nyaya Deep*, Journal of NALSAR; December, 2006; p. 68.
10. *Ibid.*
11. Nomita Agarwal, "*The Need for alternative dispute resolution in India*" , Published in the *Journal of Indian Law Institute;* Vol. 3, Dec.-2004; p. 67.
12. S. 75 of the Arbitration and Conciliation Act, 1996.
13. (2003) 1 SCC 49.
14. Justice Goda Raghuram , '*Alternative Dispute Resolution*' ; published in *Nyaya Deep,* Journal of National Legal Service Authority; Vol. VIII, April, 2007; p. 17.
15. *Ibid.*
16. *Id.*, at p. 21.
17. Ashok Agarwal; "*Mediation : Promises and Challenges*"; AIR; March 2008 (Journal Section); p. 40.
18. *Ibid.*
19. *Supra* note 14 ; at p. 21.
20. *Id.*, at p. 25.
21. Justice S.B. Sinha; "*ADR Vision 2025*" ; Published in *Nyaya Kiran*, Journal of Delhi Legal Service Authority; Jan- Mar, 2008; p. 8.
22. "European Convention On International Commercial Arbitration", 37 B.Y.I.L. 487.
23. B.S. Murphy, "*ADR's Impact on International Commerce*", *Dispute Resolution Journal* , December 1993 ,pp. 68-77.
24. Supra note- 1, at p. 35.
25. *Ibid.*
26. *Id.*, at p.36.
27. *Supra* Note 14, at p. 38.
28. *Id.*, at p. 37.
29. Mahesh Kumar, "*Lok Adalat—A Tool for ADR in India*"; published in *Nyaya Kiran*, Journal of Delhi Legal Service Authority; Vol. V, Apr.-May 2005; p. 7.
30. Art. 39A provides that the State shall secure that the operation of the legal system promotes justice, on a basis of equal opportunity and shall, in particular, provide free legal aid, by suitable legislation or schemes or in any other way, to ensure that opportunities for securing justice are not denied to any citizen by reason of economic or other disabilities.
31. (2003) 5 SCC (Journal) 43.
32. *Id.*, at p. 45.
33. N.R. Madhava Menon, "*Lok Adalat: Peoples' Programme for Speedy Justice*"; *Indian Bar Review*, Vol. 13, 1986, p. 132.
34. *Salem Advocate Bar Association, Tamilnadu* v. *Union of India*, AIR 2005 SC 3353.
35. *Supra* note 29 at p. 8.
36. Justice A.M. Ahmadi; "*Workshop on 'Lok Adalat'—An appraissal*", *Legal Aid News Letter,* Vol. XII, Apr.-June, 1992; p. 9.

37. AIR 2005 SC 3575.
38. *Ibid.*
39. Extract from Lecture delivered by Mr. K.K. Manan, Chairman Bar Council of Delhi, in the All India Seminar on Judicial Reforms in New Delhi on 25th Feb 2008.
40. Souvenir on *'All India Seminar on Access to Justice'*, Vol. 3; p. 24.
41. Black's Law Dictionary at p. 1152.
42. Justice M.Y. Eqbal,'*Concept of Plea Bargaining*' ; Published in *Nyaya Kiran*, Journal of Delhi Legal Service Authority; Vol. I, Oct.- Jan.- 2008; p. 52.
43. Ankush Bhadoriya, Plea bargaining although a new concept in India may work for speedy justice and reduce overburden of cases, Manupatra.
44. AIR 2000 (SC) 164, AIR 1999 (SCW) 4251, 2000 Cr. LJ 384.
45. AIR (2005) Cr. L.J. 2957.
46. AIR, 1976, SC 1929, 1976 Cri LJ1527.
47. AIR 1980 SC 854, 1980 Cri LJ 553.
48. *Supra* Note 45.
49. The forms of plea bargaining vary among jurisdictions. See generally Wayne R. Lafave, Jerold H. Israel & Nancy J. King, Criminal Procedure 956, 989 (3d ed. 2000). In many locales, the bargain is between the prosecution and the defence, with the judge merely exercising veto power. The bargaining may occur over the charge and over recommendations to the judge about sentencing. Alternatively, the bargaining may determine the precise sentence to be imposed, with the judge's disagreement constituting a nullification of the bargain.
50. Plea Bargaining — Is It As Consensual As Convenient? By Jasneet Kaur.
51. Plea Bargaining an analysis of the concept by Soura Shubha Ghosh.
52. India: Plea bargaining and the ghost of Malimath, A statement by the Asian Human Rights Commission, AS-163-2006, posted on 07 July 2006. AHRC is a regional non-governmental organisation monitoring and lobbying human rights issues in Asia.
53. *Id.* at p. 53.
54. See http/criminal.findlaw.com/articles/1491.html.(visited on10/05/2008)
55. *Ibid.*
56. *Supra* Note 42, at p. 67.
57. *Ibid.*
58. *Id.* at p. 316.
59. *Id.* at pp. 318-19.
60. *Id.* at p. 320.
61. *Ibid.*
62. Report was released in March 2002.
63. Recommendation No. 122 of 'National Commission to review the working of the Constitution.'
64. *Ibid.*, Recommendation No. 123.
65. *Ibid.*, Recommendation No. 124.
66. *Ibid.*, Recommendation No. 125.

67. *Ibid.*, Recommendation No. 126.
68. *Ibid.*, Recommendation No. 127.
69. *Ibid.*, Recommendation No. 128.
70. *Ibid.*, Recommendation No. 129.
71. *Ibid.*, Recommendation No. 130.
72. *Ibid.*, Recommendation No. 131.
73. *Ibid.*, Recommendation No. 132.
74. *Ibid.*, Recommendation No. 133.
75. *Ibid.*, Recommendation No. 134.
76. *Ibid.*, Recommendation No. 135.
77. *Ibid.*, Recommendation No. 136.
78. *Ibid.*, Recommendation No. 137.
79. *Ibid.*, Recommendation No. 138.
80. *Ibid*, Recommendation No. 139.
81. *Ibid.*, Recommendation No. 140.
82. *Ibid.*, Recommendation No. 141.
83. *Ibid.*, Recommendation No. 142.
84. *Ibid.*, Recommendation No. 143.
85. *Ibid.*, Recommendation No. 144.
86. *Ibid.*, Recommendation No. 145.
87. *Ibid.*, Recommendation No. 146.
88. *Ibid.*, Recommendation No. 147.
89. *Ibid.*, Recommendation No. 148.
90. *Ibid.*, Recommendation No. 149.
91. Malimath Committee's Report on Reforms in Criminal Justice System; Volume I; pp. 256-59.
92. *Id.*, at p. 262.
93. *Id.*, at p. 264.
94. The Sunday Standard, *Supreme Sacrifice for Speedy Justice,* by Kanu Sarda, New Delhi, Published: 29th Dec. 2013.
95. 14th *Report of Law Commission of India*, September 1958; Vol. I , p. 181.
96. 77th *Report of Law Commission of India*, November, 1978.
97. *Id.*, at pp. 26-30.
98. *Id.*, at p. 34.
99. *116th Report of Law Commission of India,* Nov. 1986.
100. *117th Report of Law Commission of India,* Nov. 1986, pp. 34-46.
101. *4th Report of National Police Commission of India,* pp. 23-26, June, 1980.
102. *Supra* note 78, at p. 183.
103. Report No. 239 Submitted to the Supreme Court of India in W P (C) No. 341/2004, Virender Kumar Ohri *v.* Union of India & Others, March 2012, Writ Petition (C) No. 341/2004 Virender Kumar Ohri *v.* Union of India & Others.
104. 172 (2010) *Delhi Law Times,* 268.
105. Dr. Subramanian Swamy *v.* Dr. Manmohan Singh, 2012 (2) SCALE 12.
106. 2012(2) SCALE 81.

107. AIR 2002 SC 1752, paras 24 and 25.
108. Law's Delays: Arrears in Courts (December, 2001), para 38.2.
109. Manpower Planning in Judiciary: A Blueprint (31st July, 1987), para 9.
110. W.P. (C) No. 122 of 2008.
111. C.A. No. 1867 of 2006.
112. *Supra* note 97, at 25.
113. (2006) 8SCC 1.
114. National Law News, *Quarterly Law Journal;* April, 08 June-2008.

5

Conclusion and Suggestions

CONCLUSION

To conclude the adumbration, it can be said that the values of parliamentary democracy and constitutional government committed to the principles of equity, social justice, secularism and above all, the rule of law are the very foundations on which governance must rest. To preserve and protect these vital values, the three pillars of our Republic must work together hand in hand. The institutions of governance fashioned by the founding fathers of our Republic have served us well over the last six decades. However, it is fair to state that many of the institutions have been of late showing signs of stress and today the efficiency and effectiveness of many of these institutions are being questioned. There is growing dissatisfaction regarding the functioning of the executive and the legislature due to their inability to deliver effective governance to meet the needs and challenges of our times. In this background, it is a matter of great satisfaction that the public at large continues to hold the judiciary in high esteem. The judiciary, as custodians and watchdogs of the fundamental rights of our people, is shouldering and discharging its responsibility very well indeed. But it is always wise to remain alert and watch out for the cracks and seal it swiftly. The problem of delayed disposal of cases is one of the most visible cracks and the same has reached alarming proportion during the last two decades or so.

Education is the basis of all reforms. A properly structured and suitably designed ADR Course with appropriate training and support from the bar and bench can certainly provide the opportunity to lawyers to take up the missions of implementation of ADR mechanisms. It is often said that Indian judiciary is crumbling under its own weight. It does not mean that our judicial system is ineffective. We must not forget the increased inflow of cases in all courts of the country. Litigation is not the only means of resolving disputes. We need to re-look and strengthen our own available alternative mechanisms with positive framework and proper teaching programme for law students.

It must be noted that the innovation and flexibility are the keys to solve the puzzle of such a huge backlog. The setting up of Lok Adalats has certainly provided much needed relief. It has been noted that about 95 percent cases could be solved by mediation or mutual agreement by Lok Adalat.

There is no doubt in admitting that the implementation of Alternative Dispute Resolution opens up new avenues of development. For students, Alternate Dispute Resolution mechanisms provide whole lot of new job opportunities in various spheres. Its impact on business is equally positive. Commerce is all about timely measures in the absence of which business interests of the parties are hurt. Due to globalization and liberalization, the need for speedy resolution of disputes in business is ever increasing. The confidence of business houses in law and court is eroded as courts are overburdened, which hinders speedy relief. ADR being fast and relatively inexpensive comes in handy in such situations.

The recent observations made by former Attorney General of India, Mr. Soli J. Sorabjee, that the Criminal Justice system in India is on the verge of collapse and should be taken seriously. These observations may sound exaggerated. But in the given system, which lingers on endlessly and is skewed in favour of legal professionals, these words of the former Attorney General of India may prove to be prophetic.

In every fora, seminars and symposiums relating to '**Court delays in India**', people talk of rather complain about the backlog of cases in Courts and yet strangely there is never a proper proposal made by any authority for increase in the number of Courts as an imperative to reduce the delay in delivering justice to the people. Very strangely adjournment of cases for want of time is seen as the only remedy. But this only postpones the hearing of cases causing lot of frustration to the litigant. It doesn't dispose off the case. In fact, it adds to the problem of the litigant. Everybody knows that the real solution doesn't lie in such adjournment. By adjourning cases in this manner, some cases do get automatically decided. Sometimes one or both litigants die; some times one or both litigants withdraw in sheer disgust; some times the case is dismissed because the plaintiff doesn't appear; some times the case is disposed off because the defendant is unable to appear or has died. Such extrajudicial circumstances often help to decrease the pending list of cases. But this is not judicial disposal of cases. It is often said in jest that the suit filed by a father is required to be processed by his children, the judgment is received by this grand-children and the fruits of a decree can be enjoyed only by the great grand children.

A preliminary analysis shows that increase in the number of judges required to find a solution to the problem would be at least four-fold. The recruitment of such a large number of judges may present some administrative difficulties. But those difficulties are not insurmountable. The process of recruitment of judges should not take more than six to nine months. In the meantime, infrastructure has to be kept ready for each judge—his office and staff. This has to be done with equal expediency and not neglected. It would not happen that judges are posted but corresponding offices and staffs are not provided.

A contemporary example can be cited to make this point clear. Delhi, Bombay and other cities are spending thousands of crores for constructing new highways and new malls. The railways have increased the number of zones to sixteen. But the judicial system remains where it has been for the last six decades. So, suitable highways for justice must be built. Just as new highways have to be constructed to take people from one city to the other, in the same way, adequate number of courts with adequate infrastructure should be provided for fast track finalization of all civil and criminal cases.

The Government—the Prime Minister, Chief Minister and their cabinets, to be very specific—cannot plead paucity of funds at the Union and State Level for setting up a functioning judicial system. One should remember that providing quick justice is the supreme constitutional requirement of a democracy. This is written in the preamble itself and further confirmed in various articles of the constitutions. But this fundamental requirement has all along been ignored for the last six decades. People of India have been/are crying out for justice and it is in the interest of everybody to listen to these cries and provide appropriate remedies.

So the problem of delay in disposing of cases should be nipped in the bud. If due emphasis is not given to this problem, it may have a cataclysmic effect on the whole society. If this problem is allowed to impregnate then the possibility is that the load of pending cases would be so much that we would reach a point of no return, where people would have to go away from courts without justice. The Court would become the centre of denial of justice, antithesis of what is meant for. Thus, it is an apocalypse of the eventual happening. There has to be a serious and sincere endeavor on the part of every member of the legal fraternity to annihilate the problem collectively. If this is not done on a priority basis, it would not only be the defeat of our constitutional philosophy but also contribute to the collapse of the entire judicial system.

SUGGESTIONS

A society is comprised of people and it reflects the collective ideologies of its people. Like individuals, the society also strives for progress, which can be achieved by synergetic cooperation between the citizens and those governing the society. The civil society through its executive governing body aims at an equitable distribution of resources between its members. In this process of equitable distribution, the society confers several rights to its citizens. These civil rights accrue to the citizens by virtue of they being members of the society. They stem from various obligations society has towards its members like obligations to provide proper civic amenities to the members, obligation to provide transparent and efficient governance, obligation to provide a conducive and peaceful atmosphere and so on. These civil rights are expressly or impliedly recognized in the constitutions of the countries and the laws that they enact under the authority of their constitutions in furtherance of its pursuit of idealism.

In India, civil rights are recognized in **Part III of the Constitution of India** as fundamental rights and also under various statutes enacted by the Parliament and State legislatures. Further, the constitution in its preamble solemnly declares establishment of a sovereign, socialist, secular, democratic republic and to secure all its citizens: Justice—social, economic and political; Liberty of thought, expression, belief, faith and worship and equality of status and opportunity. So, if the right of any person is infringed in any manner or there is a threat to his liberty, he must have access to justice. Speedy trial, which is implied under Art.-21 of the Indian Constitution, is one of the dimensions of access to justice. Unless there is a speedy disposal of cases, there cannot be real access to justice. Justice that comes too late has no meaning to the person it is meant for.

As we know that the formal justice delivery system in India has been cancerously sick with the well-known disease of **"delay in justice dispensation"**. Justice should not only be done but should also appear to have been done. Similarly, whereas justice delayed is justice denied, justice withheld is even worse than that. Therefore, to reduce the mounting arrears of cases and inordinate delay in disposal of cases, several initiatives have been taken from time to time but the result is not very encouraging.

After going through the pros and cons of the topic as well as the empirical study, it is expected that the following initiatives will be helpful in lessening the burdens of Courts:

1. Increasing the Number of Regular Courts

A solution to the problem can be obtained by assessing the requirements of a system which would deliver justice to a large number of litigants. The large intake of cases requires an increase in the number of courts, each with a judicial officer and corresponding infrastructure. There is also a huge backlog of pending cases and this backlog is increasing day-by-day. Each case requires a certain minimum of processing time at various levels of the court process including the time required for a judge to study the case and dispose it as per law. Such requirement of time has to be planned beforehand and infrastructure should be developed accordingly for each court. It does not appear rational that everyone keep on complaining about the backlog of cases in Courts and yet there is never a proper proposal made for increasing the number of courts to cater to the large intake of cases and pending backlog. The pending cases cannot become zero overnight and processing time for each case cannot be reduced by magic. The number of courts will have to be increased to dispose of the backlog. A system should not exist only to perpetuate itself without serving the real objective for which it is established. The judicial system should serve the useful purpose of rendering justice within a reasonable time. If people don't get their cases decided within a reasonable period of time, the system is not serving its purpose and it has to be reformed. So to dispose off the pending cases, there is a need of at least four-fold increase in the number of judicial officers.

2. Extensive Use of Emerging Technology

Dispensation of justice by adopting Information Technology has been advocated in Western Countries for the last two or three decades, but in India hardly any worthwhile effort has been made, particularly in judicial administration of subordinate courts of our country. Extensive use of Information Technology by judicial organ around the world has resulted in enhanced efficiency, effectiveness and optimal use of resources. Most of the bottlenecks identified by the judicial Commissions and Committees referring to delays, arrears and backlog can be partly tackled if a sound judicial management information system is introduced in India. Introducing new technologies, Internet facilities, video-conferencing will save the time of courts to render speedy justice. It is not enough to provide computers to the registrar and to the judges. They must know how to use the computers efficiently and effectively. There needs to be a systematic training of Court Staff in the use of computers and even for Judges who can get tremendous help from various kinds of programmes that are available on computers such as CDs of case laws, information from the internet and research facilities from specialized websites dealing with legal topics.

The increasing backlog of cases are posing a big threat to our judicial system. The same was even more in the early nineties but due to the computerization process in the Supreme Court and other courts has been reduced to a great extent. However, the backlog is still alarming. This is because mere computerization of courts or other constitutional offices will not make any difference. What we need is a will and desire to use the same for speedy disposal of various assignments. There is a lack of training among judges regarding use of Information Technology. This resource is based on the ground reality that mere computerization will not serve the purpose. As far as the computerization is concerned, the judges of all courts in Delhi have their own computers that are as per the latest configurations. However, the need of the hour is greater than mere provision of computers. For instance, there was a proposal in the Delhi High court for connecting of the computers of the concerned judges to the Central computer. Thus, whenever something is typed it would automatically go to the central computer and from there we can have the "Certified copies" of the concerned documents. This proposal has been applied to a great extent and now it is much easier to get the certified copies. Further, cause lists, name of the Judges, Courts numbers, name of the lawyers, etc. are all available on the Internet and the same has also facilitated speedier disposal of cases. However, we need more. We need a complete utilization of IT for the effective disposal of cases and witness protection. Video Conferencing has been talked about for quite some time but it is not being implemented, which is little surprising because it is one way of reducing costs, particularly in matters pertaining to under trials. If video conferencing facility is introduced, the cases can be recovered at an early date. For instance, we can use the facility of "Video Conferencing" on a large scale. Presently, it is used in some cases. We can use the medium of Internet for filing of cases, bail applications; serving of notices, etc. thus, much is still to be achieved.

3. Appointment of Judges by National Judicial Commission

Appointment of judges should be made by National Judicial Commission consisting of senior Supreme Court Judges, eminent jurists, lawyers and the law ministers in order to accelerate the process of appointments commensurate to the vacancies and avoid political arbitrariness. It is seen that the Bar Councils of most of the States make undue delay in conducting examination for appointment to the lower Judiciary. So the National Judicial Commission should regulate appointment of judges to lower, higher and specialized tribunals and such National Judicial Commission should have the power to ensure strict judicial discipline.

4. Revitalization of Judicial Academics

National Judicial Academy (NJA) has been set-up with the objective of training of judicial officers of the States, Union Territories, organizing conferences and, seminars relating to Court Management and administration of justice. Judicial academics have also been set-up in almost all states. Establishment of Judicial academies are an important step towards judicial reform but these academies need to be revitalized and the expenditure on the improvement of judicial system should be considered as an investment. Such Judicial Academies should establish **Research Centres on Judicial Reforms** including subjects such as arrears of cases.

Training of Judges at the grass root level is extremely important and if judgments at the district level are of a high quality, the number of revisions and appeals may be reduced which ultimately will reduce the arrears of cases. The Court particularly, High Courts must show initiative in this regard and try and give more strength and vigour to the Judicial Academies by holding constant programmes for training of Judicial Officers in the districts. Performance indicators have although been prepared by all High Courts but these need to be reconsidered because in some of the High Courts they are completely outdated and do not reflect ground realities.

(5) Imparting Judicial Education for better Court Management

In the concept of '**divine right of kings**', the king, who used to be considered as the incarnation of God, besides being the head of the administrative wing, the supreme commander of the armed forces, also functioned as the fountain-head of justice. The general belief for those who believed in the theory of divine right of kings was that "**king can do no wrong.**" The judges, too in the eyes of general public had a concept of divinity and the common man had such faith and belief that the judges having the concept of divinity in them knew everything on the universe and could not do any wrong. Even till the later part of 20th century, not only in our country, but in other countries like England, USA, the common view was that the judges did not require any training and their vast experience at the Bar coupled with intellect and instinct for fairness was considered enough. Educating Judges on judicial functions and training them on how to judge properly as a matter of fact are relatively new ideas which even till date are not yet accepted fully by the judicial fraternity as a whole. Some of the judges still believe that the same, in one way or the other, may amount to interference with their judicial independence whereas others resent the very idea of educating the Judges on the ground that the same amount to questioning their capacity and competence. However, with the explosion in knowledge and with the diversification of complex litigation, there has been increasing demand from many Judges themselves for the programmes of continuing education, tailored to specific problems and needs. The need for mandatory judicial education is now acknowledged throughout the world in one form or the other.

In our country, despite realizing the importance of judicial education and repeated recommendations from various Commissions and committees the pre-service institutional training to the new entrants and in-service training of Judicial Officers already in service had not received the desired attention.

The question of questions is as to why such training is necessary for judicial functionaries. Some may have a feeling that after basic routine education and professional education in Law College, coupled with some years of experience at the Bar, why should one be required to have Judicial Education. There is no doubt that a person after considerable experience at the Bar acquires that sort of legal knowledge but the fact remains that probably he would have not acquired the package of skills needed for his new role as Judge. The requirements of the job of a Judge decidedly differ substantially from that of an advocate. The judge needs to be able to preside over a courtroom, to be able to make reasoned decisions, to write a properly structured judgment and above all to listen rather than to talk. So, it is absolutely essential that a judge should fully understand the rules of procedure and evidence whether criminal or civil. He must be able to deal with disruptive people and with reluctant witnesses in his courtroom. He must have an understanding of the different ways and customs of all those who appear in front of him, whatever be their race, religion, gender, social background or state of health may be. The lack of appropriate knowledge on the part of the judge in the subject matter of his jurisdiction is bound to lead to delay and at times may even lead to a wrong exercise of discretion or a wrong decision not warranted by the facts or the law applicable leading to multiplicity of litigation.

Judicial Education has an equally important role to play in so far as a better court management is concerned. The concept of court management, though of recent origin, yet it has gained considerable importance because it has been tried and tested in many parts of the world and has been found to be a successful method of controlling the huge backlog of cases. Court management, as such, was first introduced in the United States of America in the year 1972 and over the years it has gained so much importance that now it has now become imperative for all courts to use court management techniques to reduce the caseloads. As regards our country, a lot requires to be done in the area of court management techniques.

It is high time that court management is taken out of the control of judges and entrusted to trained adjudicators who should be made accountable to the task of modernizing, maintaining and showing performance at all levels of judicial establishment. Judicial time should be devoted to judicial work only.

6. Protecting Witnesses from Turning Hostile

Witnesses turning hostile are one of the contributing factors for the delay in the expeditious delivery of justice. To protect a witness from turning hostile, the trial should be conducted in such a way that the witness does not come face-to-face with the accused, as it would help in reducing the psychological fear to a great extent. This could be done by not producing the accused in the court while the witness is deposing his testimony. Further, the name of the witnesses should not be disclosed to the accused or his lawyers. The identity of witness should be changed and he or she should be kept under special protection.

The evidence of the witness should be video recorded in front of a Magistrate or the investigating officer of the case. This video-recorded statement should be made to three authenticated copies and the original should be sealed and presented to the court as evidence. This would ensure that the witness does not retract his statement later on and would also prevent tampering of the tapes.

Sections 191-193 of the Indian Penal Code deals with perjury. As per these provisions, a witness who turns hostile shall be punished with imprisonment of either description for a term, which may extend to seven years, and shall also be liable to fine.[1] A hostile witness is no less than a rebellious violator of law. But our courts are customarily gracious to ignore or let off hostile witnesses thereby impairing the prosecution case. There may be untenable reasoning that if the hostile witnesses are taken to task by the courts, the prosecution may face more difficult situations to procure the evidence. These loose arguments cannot justify a lenient attitude towards hostile witnesses. Even in most sensational and heinous crimes like rape, murder, dacoity, etc., the conviction rate is most appalling and palpably low. Such a situation shakes confidence of the people in the judiciary. But some ray of hope has arisen after the

Zahira Sheikh's conviction for perjury. It is hoped that the courts adopt similar approach in dealing with hostile witneses.

Justice is not something which can be captured and captivated, in rigid formulae, once for all and immutability and immortality cannot be attributed to the said principles. It is a perpetual process, a complex and shifting balance between many oscillating factors. The quest for the justice has been as challenging as the quest for the holy grave and as elusive as an angelic glow. Let us endeavour to create justice, which is perceivable, permeable, and productive of values and peace in the society. Let not the stream of justice be hindered or polluted by hostility of witnesses. Let all of us work for it.

7. Reforming the Legal Education in the Country

Revamping of the legal education is another aspect, which needs to be stressed because the real answer for most legal reform lies in reforming the legal education in the country, which will ultimately lead to the improvement of the overall situation in the judiciary. The quality of legal education imparted to a student or a prospective advocate plays an important role in the sense that it is at that stage he should be motivated to perceive the profession as the one essentially meant for social and public good and that he should do everything at his command for the speedy and proper disposal of cases without being unduly influenced by his own individual interest only. Although in recent years, large number of law schools have mushroomed in every state, but the quality of legal education imparted in these schools is pathetic and it does not match upto the challenges of the profession. Some reforms aimed at improving the legal education have been undertaken recently in the country, but much remains to be done.

Money spent on improving the legal education should be considered as an investment. In this regard the Bar Council's proposal to shut down all the evening Law Colleges and close down three-year law courses in favour of five year integrated law courses should be deliberated upon seriously. There is an eminent need to improve the quality of persons entering the legal profession. Appropriate filters in the form of strict qualification examinations for entry into law colleges and the Bar should be put in place so as to ensure that only the very best find their place in the legal profession and not those for whom there is no hope in any other profession.

OTHER SUGGESTIONS

Apart from the above, the following suggestions may be considered:

- In a vast majority of cases, adjournments are taken on false pretexts, and the law does not have any appropriate method to tackle them. A strict view on adjournments is required.
- Every transfer of a judge involves repetitive and wasteful procedures which involve delays, deceleration in the process of disposal and unwanted adjournments. So the procedure regarding transfer should be made as simple as it can be within the shortest possible time.
- Once a trial court completes recording of evidence and hearing of arguments of advocates, it should be made mandatory for the judge to deliver the judgment within a maximum time limit of 30 days thereafter.
- A provision can be made to have sittings of Magistrates within the prison premises. It would not only save time but would also avoid bringing the accused to courts by hand cuffing etc.
- Serving summons and warrant notices is another area which takes a lot of time. So to reduce time-consumption, modern gadgets such as phones, wireless systems, fax machines, internet facilities connected with police headquarters should be accepted as valid mode and should be made accessible to both Civil and Criminal Courts so that summons and notices can be sent faster.
- No oral evidence be insisted where matter rests solely on documentary evidence.
- Evidence should be tape-recorded or recorded by short-hand stenographers and a verbatim record should be kept in the Court which can be used while delivering decisions.
- At least for two years all the vacations i.e., summer vacation, winter vacation, puja vacation, etc. should be terminated as a special case to dispose off the cases and also judges should sit for the whole day so that the maximum number of cases can be disposed off.
- Avoid double numbering system of proceedings, i.e. first

time inward entry should be the final number of the proceeding as it will save time.

- Reduce pre-trial scrutiny only to verify payment of proper court fees and other objections to be taken up by other side and fix a time limit.
- Preparation and service of Summons should be allowed mainly through Advocates.
- Emphasis has to be given on final disposal of matters than on disposing interim applications and, therefore, interlocutory orders should be an exception rather than the rule. Interim orders should not result in prolongation of the case.
- In recording the plea of the accused, answers to each allegation should be recorded.
- Where an Advocate is appointed, presence of parties should be insisted upon only at crucial stages of trial.
- Copies of Judgments should be given in open court to parties.
- Lengthy judgments should be avoided.
- Supreme Court and High Court decisions ought to be published by those Courts just as the Acts and Rules published by the Government, since those decisions are constitutionally binding on lower Courts.
- Arbitration procedure should be made applicable to all courts and all complicated civil and criminal procedures which are the root cause of the delays should be abolished.
- Set up more specialized tribunals and reduce load on courts and introduce shift system in courts.
- There must be a process of progressive and massive discriminalization of offences now recognized and made culpable as penal offences. They should be treated as merely actionable wrongs for which compensation and not punitive action is the appropriate remedy.
- The class of compoundable offences under the Indian Penal Code (IPC) and other laws should be widened.
- In the disposal of arrears of criminal cases, experienced criminal lawyers be requested to work as part-time judges on a particular stipulated number of days on the pattern of 'Records and Assistant Records' in the United Kingdom. There is an existing provision in the Criminal Procedure

Code for honorary Judicial Magistrates, which has not been utilized or its potential realized even in part.

- Magistrates and Sessions Judges while remanding person under trial to judicial custody should clearly indicate in the very order of remand the date of termination of the same. That is, the judicial remands should be self-limiting and should indicate the date on which the under-trial prisoner would automatically be entitled to get bail in terms of the conditions prescribed by the Supreme Court.
- There should be a comprehensive training package or programmes of training of all judicial personnel and Court administration.
- In the proportion of population-judge ratio, India is today amongst lowest in the world; this needs to be rectified.
- The right to appeal against interim and interlocutory orders should be curtailed because these are normally ploys to prolong the cases. Only summary appeals should be allowed. Further the overall appeal procedures should be made strict.
- Arrears before every judge should be made public every 6 months and the Chief Justice should be given power to discipline judges who is found to be dragging the cases.
- Judiciary should be made part of the plan so that there are more Courts, judges and law-clerks to assist the judiciary.
- Written brief should be made the norm and oral arguments should be minimal and time-bound.
- There is a need for a geographical decentralization of the judicial structure. Considering the enormous size of the country and the inconvenience caused to the litigants coming from remote corners of the country — a Supreme Court bench be attached with every High Court and a High Court bench be attached with every district Court.
- Fast Track Courts should be treated as different from normal Courts and should be given very specific matters to handle. Over burdening would lead them handling an equal amount of litigation. Such Courts should only be given old pending matters or matters which are very complicated or the disposal of which require a large number of witnesses.

Let me conclude the adumbration by quoting Justice **Warren Burger**, the former Chief Justice of American Supreme Court. He had observed and I quote:

> "The harsh truth is that we may be on our way to a society overrun by hordes of lawyers, hungry as locusts and bridges of judges in numbers never before contemplated. The notion that ordinary people want black robed judges, well-dressed lawyers, fine paneled Court-rooms as the setting to resolve their disputes, is not correct. People with legal problems like people with pain, want relief and they want it as quickly and inexpensively as possible."

Note

1. Sec. 193, Indian Penal Code.

APPENDIX

SCHEDULE FOR INTERVIEW OF LITIGANTS

1. Do you have any case pending in any Court?
2. What is the nature of the pending case?
3. When was the case filed against you or by you?
4. What is the status/stage of the case?
5. What are the reasons for delay in the disposal of cases?
6. What do you think is the main reason for delay in the disposal of cases?

SCHEDULE FOR INTERVIEW OF LAWYERS

1. What kind of cases are you dealing in?
2. When did you join the profession?
3. What do you think is the main reason for delay in the disposal of cases?
4. What is your personal experience on delay?
5. What is the maximum time taken in a case dealt by you?

SCHEDULE FOR INTERVIEW OF JUDICIAL OFFICER

1. What is the designation of the Judicial Officer?
2. For how many years he has been serving as a Judicial Officer ?
3. What do you think is the main reason for delay in the disposal of cases?

Bibliography

ARTICLES

Ahmadi, A.M.; "*Lok Adalat: An Appraissal*"; *Legal Aid News Letter*, Vol. XII; Apr.-June, 1992.

Agarwal, B.N.; *Mediation: "Promises and Challenges"*; AIR, March 2008 (Journal Section).

Bhariok, Neora; "*Balancing between Speedier and Fair Justice*"; *Delhi Law Review*, Vol. XXVII; 2005.

Bishwal, Acharya; "*Speedy Justice by the Use of Technology*"; Souvenir on All India Seminar on Judicial Reforms held on 23rd-24th Feb, 2008.

Chelliah, A.E.; *"Speeding up of Justice Delivery System with Special Reference to Procedural Reforms and Use of Technology in case Management".*

Dalal, Pravin; *Right to Speedy Trial*; Souvenir on All India Seminar on Judicial Reforms held on 23rd-24th Feb. 2008.

Dave, D. Suchit; "*Speeding up of Justice Delivery System with Special Reference to Procedural Reforms and Use of Technology in case Management*" Souvenir on All India Seminar on Judicial Reforms held on 23rd-24th Feb. 2008.

Deshpande, R.R.; *"Reform in the Criminal Justice System—Pre-trial, During the trial Publicity";* Souvenir on All India Seminar on Judicial Reforms held on 23rd-24th Feb., 2008.

Diwan, Paras; "Justice at the Doorstep of the People: The Lok Adalat System"; AIR Aug. 1991 (Journal Section).

Eqbal, M.Y.; "*Concept of Plea Bargaining*"; Published in *Nyaya Deep*; Journal of National Legal Service Authority.

George, Julien; "*Legal Education-Keeping Pace with Latest Development*".

Khanna, Kishan; "*Justice Delayed Is Justice Denied*"; Souvenir on All India Seminar on Judicial Reforms held on 23rd-24th Feb. 2008.

Kumar, Mahesh; "*Lok Adalat, a tool for ADR in India*"; Published in *Nyaya Kiran*, Journal of Delhi Legal Service Authority; Apr.-June, 2005.

Mathur, A.N.; "*Future of Plea Bargaining*", AIR March 2003 (Journal Section).

Menon, Madhava; "*Lok Adalat: People's Programmes for Speedy Justice*"; *Indian Bar Review*, Vol. XIII, 1986.

Prasad, Lokeshwar; "*Judicial Education for Arrears Reduction and Better Court Management*"; AIR, Apr. 2001 (Journal Section).

Qureshi, A.R.; "*Court Vacation and Law Delays*"; Souvenir on All India Seminar on Judicial Reforms held on 23rd-24th Feb, 2008.

Seth, J.C.; "*Efficacy of Arbitration*"; *Nyaya Deep*, Journal of National Legal Service Authority; Apr.-June 2005.

Siddiqui, Shawahiq and Abbasi, Yassir; "*Speeding up of Justice Delivery System with Special Reference to Procedural Reforms and Use of Technology in case Management*". Souvenir on All India Seminar on Judicial Reforms held on 23rd-24th Feb. 2008.

Sinha, S.B.; "*ADR Vision 2025*"; AIR, Dec. 2002 (Journal Section).

Singh, Prakash; "*Legal Education—Keeping Pace with Latest Development*". Souvenir on All India Seminar on Judicial Reforms held on 23rd-24th Feb, 2008.

Jayanth K. Krishnan and C. Raj Kumar, "Delay in Process, Denial of Justice: The Jurisprudence and Empirics of Speedy Trials in Comparative Perspective", *Georgetown Journal of International Law,* 2011, Vol. 42.

BOOKS

Arora, B.L.; *Law of Speedy Trial in India*; 1st Edition, 2005; Universal Law Publishing Co. Pvt. Ltd.

Ashok A. Desai; *Justicing the People*; 2nd edition, 2001; Modern Law House.

Bakshi, Upendra; "*Right to Speedy Trial: Geese, Gender And Judicial Sauce*"; 2nd ed., 1986.

C.K. Thakwani; *Civil Procedure Code*; 5th Edition, 2003; Eastern Book Company, Lucknow.

Cyrus Das and K. Chandra; *Judges and Judicial Accountability*; 2nd Edition, 2005; Universal Law Publishing Co. Pvt. Ltd.

Gokulesh Sharma; *Select World Constitution;* 1st Edition, 2004, Vol. I; Deep and Deep Publication Pvt. Ltd.

Gokulesh Sharma; *Human Rights and Social Justice*; 2nd Edition, 2003; Deep and Deep Publication Pvt. Ltd.

H.M. Seervai; *Constitutional Law of India*; 3rd Edition, 2001; Universal Law Publishing Co. Pvt. Ltd.

J.N. Pandey; *Constitutional Law of India*; 42nd Edition, 2005; Central Law Agency, Allahabad.

J.S. Verma; *New Dimensions of Justice;* 2nd Edition, 2003; Universal Law Publishing Co. Pvt. Ltd.

M.P. Jain; *Constitutional Law of India*; 3rd Edition, 2001; Modern Law House.

M.V. Pylee; *Constitutions of the World;* 2000 Edition; Universal Law Publishing Co. Pvt. Ltd.

R.C. Lahoti; *Preamble–the Spirit and Backbone of the Constitution of India*; 1st Edition, 2004; Eastern Book Company, Lucknow.

R.V. Kelkhar; *Criminal Procedure Code* revised by K.M.C. Pillai; 4th Edition, 2001, Reprinted in 2004; Eastern Book Company, Lucknow.

S.N. Mishra; *The Code of Criminal Procedure*; 11th Edition, 2004; Central Law Publications.

Upendra Baxi*; The Crisis of the Indian Legal System*; 1st Edition, 1980; Vikash Publication, New Delhi.

V.R. Krishna Iyer; *Judges' Potpourri;* 3rd Edition, 2007; Universal Law Publishing Co. Pvt. Ltd.

Granville Austin, Working A Democratic Constitution: The Indian Experience (1999).

Upendra Baxi, The Indian Supreme Court and Politics (Eastern Book Co.) (1980).

Rajeev Dhavan, The Supreme Court of India: A Socio-Legal critique of its Juristic Techniques (1977).

S.P. Sathe, Judicial Activism in India: Transgressing Borders and Enforcing Limits (New Delhi: Oxford University Press) (2002).

BARE ACTS

The Code of Civil Procedure.
The Code of Criminal Procedure.
The Indian Evidence Act.
The Indian Penal Code.

JOURNAL

Amity Law Watch.
Delhi Judicial Academy Law Journal.
Delhi Law Review.
International Council of Arbitration Quarterly.
Journal of Indian Law Institute, New Delhi.
Journal, All India Reporters.
JUSTITIA, Osmania University Law Journal.
Law Review, National University of Juridical Science, kolkata.
Maharshi Dayanand University (MDU) Law Journal.
Practical Lawyer, The Edited by Surendra Malik.
Vidyasthali Law Journal.
Vidhigya—The Journal of Legal Awareness. Published from Integrated School of Law, Ghaziabad.
National Law News, Quarterly Law Journal; April 08-June 08.
Georgetown Journal of International Law, 2011, Vol. 42.

REPORTS

Report of Law Commission of India on Expeditious Investigation and Trial of Criminal Cases against Influential Public Personalities Report No. 239 Submitted to the Supreme Court of India in WP (C) No. 341/2004, March 2012.

Crimes in India, 2010 Statistics, published by National Crime Records Bureau, Ministry of Home Affairs, Government of India.

Chief Justice K.G. Balakrishnan, "All India Seminer on Judicial Reform" held from 23rd - 25th Feb. 2008 in New Delhi.

MAGAZINES

Competition Success Refresher.
The Frontline.
India Today.
The Rational.
Lawyers Update.

WEBSITES

www.amnesty.org.in
www.blonnet.Com
www.criminalfindlaw.com
www.frontline.net.in
www.google.com
www.indiatoday.com
www.legalservicesindia.com
www.manupatra.com

Index